ON NATIVE GROUND

American Indian Literature and

Critical Studies Series

Gerald Vizenor and Louis Owens, General Editors

ON NATIVE GROUND
Memoirs and Impressions

By Jim Barnes

UNIVERSITY OF OKLAHOMA PRESS: NORMAN AND LONDON

Also by Jim Barnes

The Fish on Poteau Mountain (Mason City, Iowa, 1980)
The American Book of the Dead (Champaign, Ill., 1982)
A Season of Loss (West Lafayette, Ind., 1985)
La Plata Cantata (West Lafayette, Ind., 1989)
The Sawdust War (Champaign, Ill., 1992)
Paris (Champaign, Ill., 1997)

Some of the prose sections in this volume are reprinted from *I Tell You Now: Autobiographical Essays by Native American Writers*, edited by Brian Swann and Arnold Krupat, by permission of the University of Nebraska Press. Copyright © 1987 by the University of Nebraska Press. The poems "Flugwetter," "Flug," "Vorgefühl," "Am Ufer," and "Abschiede" are printed in this volume by permission of Dagmar Nick.

On Native Ground is Volume 23 in the American Indian Literature and Critical Studies Series.

Text design by Debora Hackworth.

Library of Congress Cataloging-in-Publication Data

Barnes, Jim, 1933–
    On native ground: memoirs and impressions / by Jim Barnes.
        p.   cm. — (American Indian literature and critical studies series; v. 23)
    ISBN 0–8061–2898–4 (alk. paper)
    1. Barnes, Jim, 1933–   —Biography. 2. Poets, American—20th century—Biography. 3. Indians of North America—Biography. 4. Indians of North America—Poetry.   I. Title.   II. Series.
    PS3552.A67395Z472   1997
    811'.54—dc20
    [B]   96–36292
                                                                              CIP

The paper in this book meets the guidelines for permanence and durability of the Committee on Production Guidelines for Book Longevity of the Council on Library Resources, Inc.♾

Copyright © 1997 by Jim Barnes. Published by the University of Oklahoma Press, Norman, Publishing Division of the University. All rights reserved. Manufactured in the U.S.A.
1 2 3 4 5 6 7 8 9 10

To Carolyn, now and always

We do understand so little of what is really happening to us in any given moment. Only by remembering, comparing, waiting to know the consequences can we sometimes, in a flash of light, see what a certain event really meant, what it was trying to tell us. So this will be notes on a fateful thing that happened to me when I was young and did not know much about the world or about myself.

—Katherine Anne Porter, "St. Augustine and the Bullfight"

Il ne s'agit pas ici de clabauder sur moi-même et sur mes amis; je n'ai pas le goût des potinages. Je laisserai résolument dans l'ombre beaucoup de choses.

—Simone de Beauvoir, *La force de l'âge*

ACKNOWLEDGMENTS

Many of the poems included in this volume appeared in previously published books, as follows:

The Fish on Poteau Mountain (Cedar Creek Press, 1980): "Domain," "Going up Deadman's Trail," "Wolf Hunting Near Nashoba," "Goshen Tavern," "Looking for Arrowheads," and "On Blue Mountain Tower."

Summons and Sign: Poems by Dagmar Nick (The Chariton Review Press, 1980): "Vorgefühl," "Presentiment," "Abschiede," and "Farewells."

The American Book of the Dead (University of Illinois Press, 1982): "The Exact Center of the World," "On the Bridge at Fourche Maline River," "Autobiography: Last Chapter," "Elegy for the Girl Who Drowned at Goats Bluff," "My Father's House," "Autobiographical Flashback: Puma and Pokeweed," "Autobiography, Chapter XIII: Ghost Train, the Dream," "Scouting Tom Fry Hollow," "An Ex-Deputy Sheriff Remembers the Eastern Oklahoma Murderers," "The Family Plot," "Autobiography, Chapter V: Ghost Town," "Under Buffalo Mountain," "Origin," "Autobiography, Chapter I: Leaving Summerfield," "Autobiography, Chapter XIV: Tombstone at Petit Bay, near Tahlequah," "The Body Falters," and "Autobiography, Chapter VII: Home for Memorial Day."

A Season of Loss (Purdue University Press, 1985): "The Drowning," "Heartland," "Rabbits," Rest Stop at Horse Thief Spring," "Halcyon Days," "Dog Days," "On the Mountain," "In Memory of a Day Nobody Remembers: 26 September 1874," "The Sentence," and "The Captive Stone."

La Plata Cantata (Purdue University Press, 1989): "Touching the Rattlesnake," "Hunting Winding Stair Mountain," and "The Game."

The Sawdust War (University of Illinois Press, 1992): "Crow White," "On Hearing the News That Hitler Was Dead," "The Sawdust War," "Written during the Funeral of Hirohito," "Under the Tent," "The Ranch, Wild Horse Canyon, 1943," "For Roland, Presumed Taken," "Skipping," "Legacy of Bones," "After the Great Plains," "Francesca e Paolo: Bellagio," "In Another Country," "Castle Keep," "South Wind," "Mule Track to Suira," "To Loppia," "In the Melzi Gardens," "In the Formal Garden," "The Frati: Crypt, Chapel, Oboe," and "Regatta."

Paris (University of Illinois Press, 1997): "Poem on His Birthday," "At the Festival de Poésie," "Passerelle Debilly," "One O'Clock in the Morning," "Finding Oscar Wilde," "Lovers, Light, November Rain," "Near Proust's Apartment," "Upstairs at Café de Flore," "By the Seine, a Promise," "At the Coupole," "At the Tomb of Baudelaire," "Meeting Susan S. at Musée de l'Orangerie," "In Café des Deux Cascades d'Aise," "Looking for Hemingway's Ghost at the Crillon," "Shakespeare & Co.," "114 Boulevard St. Germain," "After the Parade," "On Rue de Fleurus," "Marlene Dietrich Est Morte," "Place des Vosges," "Quasimodo's Bell," "Vision and Prayer," "Mirabeau Bridge," "Boating the Seine," "Rodin's Garden," "Fireworks over Parc Monceau," "Crown," "Fall in the Tuileries," "American Poet," "Surrealist Poet," "Bequest: Coat to the Pompidou," "Celebration," "Alpine Idyll," and "Lamentation and Farewell."

Of the poems in "Paris," many have appeared in the following journals: *American Literary Review, Anemone, Artful Dodge, Artis* (Paris), *Callaloo, Confrontation, The Formalist, Georgia Review, The Gettysburg Review, Green Mountains Review, Hurakan, The Indiana Review, The Laurel Review, Licking River Review, The Midwest Quarterly, The Nebraska Review, New Jersey Review, New Letters, Nimrod, Ohio Review, Onthebus, Paintbrush, Portlander, Prairie Schooner, Quarterly West, Rain City Review, The Sewanee Review, The South Dakota Review, Southern Humanities Review, Spoon River Poetry Review,* and *West Branch.*

Some of the prose sections in this volume appeared in *I Tell You Now: Autobiographical Essays by Native American Writers,* edited by Brian Swann and Arnold Krupat, University of Nebraska Press, copyright © 1987 by the University of Nebraska Press, and in the following journals: *Snowy Egret, North American Review, Margins* (United Kingdom), *Nimrod,* and *The Midnight Lamp.*

A special word of thanks is due to The Camargo Foundation, Cassis, France, for the 1996 fellowship that allowed the author time to make significant revisions in the manuscript for this book.

ON NATIVE GROUND

I was five years old the last time I heard the mountain lion scream.

That was in Oklahoma, 1938, when times were hard and life was good—and sacred. But a year later the WPA had done its work: roads were cut, burial mounds were dug into, small concrete dams were blocking nearly every stream. The government was caring for its people. Many were the make-work jobs. A man could eat again, while all about him the land suffered. The annual spring migration of that lone panther was no more. The riverbanks that had been his roads and way stations bore the scars of the times, the scars of loss.

In my mind the rivers must always run free. But in truth today I do not recognize them. They are alien bodies on a flattening land where everything has been made safe, civilized into near extinction. Sounds of speedboats drown out the call of the remaining jays and crows. The din of highway traffic carries for miles now that the timber has fallen to chain saw or chemical rot. Green silence in the heavy heat of summer afternoons is no more.

The Fourche Maline River and Holson Creek flow through much of what I have written. I suspect they were always there, even back in the mid-1950s when I wrote my first bad short story and my first bad verse. My sense of place is inexorably linked to these two streams and to the prairies and woods between them.

I was born within spitting distance of the Fourche Maline, on a meadow in a house that no longer stands. A lone clump of gnarled sassafras and oak rises out of the meadow a short mile northeast of Summerfield, in the hill country of eastern Oklahoma, where the land was once heavy with wood and game. Nobody knows why the clump of trees was not cut down when the land was first cleared for the plow. Once there was a house a few feet east of the trees. The broken tile of a well long since filled still rises a few inches above the earth. But you have to look long, for the tall grass hides it like the night. I cannot remember a time when the house stood there. My mother said that, as a child a few months old, she lived there for a short while at the turn of the century when her parents first moved up from Texas. But she did not recall the house, nor why it is no more.

Maybe the maker of the house knew why the trees were left in the middle of the field. At any rate, the trees are still there and are not threatened. Local legend has it that they once guarded a rich burial mound, but now no mound rises among the trees. Instead, a musky sink in the middle of the clump shows the scars of many a shovel and many a firelit night. The story of one night in particular sticks in my mind, though I was much too young at the time to know of the night at all. But like bedtime ghost stories, some things told again and again when you are young and lying with your brothers and sisters on a pallet before the hearth of the fireplace later illuminate the dim, unremembered years. It is the story of how my brother outran a horse.

Before I could stand alone, we lived on the lane that borders the east edge of the field where the trees still stand.

My brother was nearing manhood and owned a horse and was a night rider. He learned that three men, neighbors and good-for-nothings, planned to dig in the trees. He asked to join them. He longed to prove himself a man. They had visions of gold and told him there was money buried there.

So when the October moon was dark, they gathered in the clump of trees and hung a lantern over the chosen spot. There was frost on the limbs of the sassafras and oaks. My brother broke first ground, and a hushed moan moved through the still trees. He dropped the shovel; later, strange pieces of bone-red matter began to show up in the dirt at the edge of the pit. While all were gathered about, another moan, much louder than the first, moved through the night—and my brother leaped out of the dark pit. But the good-for-nothings held him fast and howled with laughter as one of their cronies strode into the circle of the lantern's light, drunk on erupting mirth and bootleg whiskey. Everyone had a good laugh at my brother's expense. And he laughed too.

But the laughter was short-lived. A deep, low moan— ghostly but unmistakably human—rolled up from the bowels of the black earth. For a moment, my brother recalls, a stillness like doom hung upon all of them. Then everybody was running, running: the good-for-nothings were running, the original moaner was running, my brother was running, and all the beasts of the field. A great shadow passed beside my brother. It was a horse. The moan persisted, even over the sound of thumping boots and racing hoofs. Now my brother passed the horse and burst through the barbed wire fence at the edge of the field with one wild bound. He flung himself down the lane and plunged through the doorway of our house and hugged himself close to the dying coals in the fireplace. An hour passed before he began to cry.

Several days later my father filled in the pit and brought home the lantern, dry of kerosene, the wick burned to a crisp.

The clump of trees in the middle of the field was the hub of the universe of my childhood and my adolescence. We always lived within sight of the field. And after the field became a great meadow, I found several days of bone-breaking work each summer helping a cousin bale the tall and fragrant lespedeza that had been urged to grow there. But never did I seek the shade of those trees for my noonday rest. For me, they were too ghostly, foreboding, sacred. In my mind's eye I could see beyond all doubt that here was the final resting place of the broken bones of some great Choctaw chief. He had made it just this far west. He had come within sight of the blue Kiamichi range to the south, which was to become the last home for his dispossessed people, and had fallen dead on the spot from a homesickness of the soul. Among the sassafras and oaks he had been buried with all the pomp and honor that was left to his migrating children. For me, the spot was inviolate.

And thus it has remained. Only recently have I had the courage, and the reverence, to penetrate the gnarled clump of trees in the middle of the meadow. I went there in midafternoon and sat as motionless as I could while the sun dropped well below a long, low line of trees far to the west. Sitting there, I tried to grasp something I could not name, something I knew as gone forever. I could not invoke it. I did not know its name. Once, just as the sun went down, I heard a hawk cry out high above the clump of leafless trees. Perhaps there was a moan. But I did not hear it.

The Exact Center of the World

The owl among the trees screaming
like a mad mother's ghost is gone.
The mound of the guarding owl has sunk,
its skull nearly level with the ground.
The stones move in. A new forest

in twisted form crawls to the place
you found hard midnight at fifteen:
heard the screech owl scream, the moon fall,
and the breaking of ancestral bones.

Here you knew a first real fear and ran
past the second wind you never felt.
Dark times. But now the moon is back
and your eyes clear in the chalk of night.
Now you know all the ghosts are dead,
except the one never laid to rest:
this mound in this clearing is the exact
center of the world. All things move round
it. And here sundown explains nothing.

Named by the French who early explored eastern Oklahoma, the Fourche Maline is by literal definition and personal observation a dirty stream, though one which once
teemed with all the life that water could possibly bear. It
was home to some of the world's largest catfish. I have seen
mudcat and shovelbill taken from the river, on bank hooks
or trotlines, huge fish that ran to more than a hundred
pounds each, their hides so scarred and tough you had to
skin them with wire pliers or Vise-Grips. Bullfrogs loud
enough to drown a rebel yell, turtles big as washtubs, and
cottonmouths all called it home, dared you to enter their
domain. I can remember bear tracks on the shoals, mussel
shells bitten in half.

The Fourche Maline was always a sluggish river, at least
for the last twenty-five miles of its course. Though its head
is in the western end of the Sans Bois mountain range, where
ridges are still thick with government-protected scrub pine
and savannah sandstone, and the water begins pure and
clear, it is soon fed by farms and ranches with runoff from

cornfields and feedlots and by worked-out coal mines as it snakes its way eastward to join Holson Creek. I can recall a time when the Fourche Maline cleared in early summer even as far as its mouth, and the water of the deep pools tasted of springs. Now the river runs ever more slowly, if at all. Its life grows stagnant out of season.

Conversely, Holson Creek—named for Holson Valley, from which it heads northward—was in the past a clear, fast-running stream. It flowed through the pines of Winding Stair and Blue mountains, through pastureland thick with native grasses, among stones that seem still today old as the sky. When I remember Holson Creek as it was in my youth, I can smell the odor of water willows, sharp in the summer, and hear the sounds of barking squirrels, of rapids and small falls, the banks rich with a treasure of arrowheads.

But now both rivers are slow, dammed. Where they meet, mouth to mouth, a lake begins. And for miles back up both streams it is difficult for the eye to discern movement of water, except in flood time, and then there is no guarantee which way they may run.

The land and streams are changing. Even what is protected pollutes: in the wildlife refuge, near the confluence of the Fourche Maline and the Holson, there are so many deer now that tick fever has thinned even the equalizing coyotes and has put salt fear into the veins of poachers, who once knew—who once were, right along with the coyotes— the true balancing force in nature.

Though fishing is sometimes fair, gone are the days of the scream of the mountain lion, the days of the big catfish. No one has seen a bear track in forty years. I doubt you could get snakebitten if you wanted to. But I am a child of the past. I live it in my waking dreams. The white clay banks along the Fourche Maline still hold their lure and the lore I assigned to them. I dug caves there. I danced the old songs.

I attacked wagon trains or, on the other side, killed Indians. And once in a rare sundown, I realized that here in the bottomland stood the only native holly tree I knew of anywhere in the great wooded valleys between the Sans Bois mountains to the north and the blue Kiamichi to the south. The holly tree is gone, victim of the backwater of the Corps of Engineers. When backwater rises, is held like a cesspool for weeks on end, all flora and fauna rooted to place die. Even a simple child knows this.

What's more, and the hell of it all: I see but little hope, rather mainly dissolution of river, of land, and thus of spirit. You can see it plain on the faces of those who have witnessed, have lived, these civilizing years. Their faces are not lined without cause; there is something in the blood that needs rivers free, forests and prairies green with promise. Maybe lack of fuel and the death of automobiles will help, but I doubt it: I know people who will hike ten miles or more carrying a six-pack just to be able to throw the emptied cans into a stream to see how long they will stay afloat while they are pumped full of lead.

We have been called a nation of tourists. But I suspect, deep down, that some of us somehow know where home is—and what it has become.

On the Bridge at Fourche Maline River

Forty feet below, the water stands as dull
as dog days. No movement toward the lake
ten snaking miles away. You stand here full
of hope you have always been told to have,
with no regard for the ruined years, those rabid
foxes at your heels.

              You stop here whenever
you have the time. The river's pull is strong.

The dark water, too thick and slow to reflect
anything outside itself, sends a constant song.
Worlds away you always know the river
is your home. You've never seen the river
run toward its sea. Yet it moves at the touch
when you take time to go down, lay your hands
on the warm river, and speak to the current
that flows into and through your blood.

                                        It has
been years since you swam this muddy stream
and, bearing a rock for ballast, walked the bottom
straight across, bank to bank, in the longest breath
you ever held. Time and time again, as now,
you dream that walk. This time it's real. You leave
your clothes flapping on the rail and jump, wide,
into the warm water and feel the river
bottom wrap a gentle skin about your feet.
As you break upward for breath, you taste
the sweet meat of earth the river is made of,
and you remember the earth and that you are home.

At the end of summer, when the apples began to turn from green to red, for a period of some two or three years in my early adolescence, an undeniable wanderlust seized me. It remains as inexpressible as a drunken dream, except in certain concrete terms. That feeling of longing, in the dull hours between dusk and bedtime when there was nothing to do except wander the roads, has long been the source of solid fiction on the one hand and sloppy sentimentalism on the other.

Many of those hours I spent in the company of three friends of like mind, if you could say we had minds then. Our admitted problem was that there was nothing to do in and around Summerfield. We were bored with our little lives. Of course we dreamed, but those dreams could not be spoken of without weakening our image, though we were much too young to know what our image was.

The apple raids were our answer to the nothingness that we inhabited, or the nothingness that inhabited us. The two "orchards" that were our objectives for two or three summers lay at opposite ends of the town, which itself consisted of two general stores and one gas station. One night in that last summer, in early September before our school began,

the four of us—Chief, Sundance, Itchy Boy, and I—decided
to raid Hosey Austin's orchard, a lone apple tree in the
middle of a small meadow just off the road a mile south of
town. That tree, we knew, was loaded with McIntoshes the
size of our fists. We galumphed down the road with all the
grace of a herd of steers, but grew more cautious when we
climbed the fence that separated the road from the meadow.
We filled our shirts with the ripening fruit, keeping a sharp
eye on Hosey's house and the light in the kitchen window.
Thieves in the night, we assumed our mist of invisibility.
We were Robin Hoods all, and we gave to ourselves the
bounty of the night.

A car door slammed and an engine started. Then Hosey's
old green Ford nosed into the road toward town. I don't
remember who threw the first apple, perhaps Chief, that
wild Choctaw, perhaps Itchy Boy, but it was a kerthunking
bull's-eye. All of us followed suit, pelting the car from beyond the barbed wire fence. It all happened in the space
of perhaps three seconds. Then we ran, in all our terrible
innocence, exploding through the night with howling laughter that would have awakened the dead. We must have run
two miles into the hills before we became brave enough to
stop. Where we had gone no man could have followed. Safe
among the pines and blackjack oaks of the westernmost
reaches of Nanny Ridge, we relished the misery of the old
green Ford. We relished the great risk we had run. We had
attempted the Golden Fleece and won it, we had insulted
the Sheriff of Nottingham, we had outrun Geronimo.

But still the night was young, and we were full of pith
and vinegar. Surely another adventure lay before us. We
decided to follow our old routine and raid H. C. Coleman's
small apple patch north of town. There was no real risk to
run there, since H. C.'s eight or ten apple trees were hidden
from view of his house by surrounding woods and were

well off the road. But his apples were big ones, the size of softballs, and still growing. As objects of the night quest, they were worthy beyond anything else we could imagine.

Regardless of the dark and our relative security, we approached the small orchard warily, perhaps because of some beginning glimmer of guilt. Itchy Boy had just begun to climb the briar-laden fence near the bordering trees when we heard something not quite belonging to the night. We shushed him back down and listened. Groans from the orchard reached us, a strangely urgent whispering-groaning. I felt the hair rise on the nape of my neck. I remembered many a ghost story told at hearthside when the moon was down. Sundance shied backward a few steps and said he had to go home because Pearl and Dooley would whip the tar out of him if he stayed out too late. Chief told him to shush and listen.

Itchy Boy started snaking along the fencerow. We followed on more than little cats' feet. This was something different; this was *the* adventure. He halted, where the briars on the fence thinned out, and lay prone on the dark grass. We joined him, not knowing what to expect. The moon began to rise, huge above the treeline at our backs. We could make out the apple trees shimmering in their cleared space and, beneath one of them, the faint white outline of two human forms.

The whiteness of the bodies shocked us. The groaning grew louder, the whispering more urgent. It was slow to dawn upon us—that act of love or lust. But when we realized what it was, we rose as one and slowly walked away without a word, each going to his own true place in the night, the mystery surrounding us, revealed to us. Each in his own way would consider the mystery of human copulation. We did not know how we were supposed to feel or react: no one had told us. We felt only that we knew nothing of the night.

Days later we all joked about what we darkly had seen, but there was still an air of mystery about it we could not in all our waning innocence name. We never learned who the copulating bodies were, nor did it really matter. What mattered was the terrible innocence we had felt that night and lost. Thereafter whenever we roamed the roads, woods, fields, it was never quite the same. A certain joy had come with the night; a certain joy had gone. We had had a vision of beginnings, and we had tasted the fruit, and now we had to survive the fierce vicissitudes of youth.

Since that last summer, I have never spoken of the night with Chief, Sundance, or Itchy Boy. We have all drifted pretty much our separate ways—through high school, through college, through wives, mortgages, deaths. But now, though I can rationalize nearly everything away, a sense of loss that was gain takes hold of me when I remember the night of the apple raids. All memory pales beside it. The white forms in the moonlight straining beneath the apple trees remain a sustaining vision of beginnings, of when we were young and reckless and fierce with determination to fire our little lives with meaning that we would surely some-day understand.

Domain

The hawk sweeps in on a wing of the sun,
brakes to a stop, trembling and still,
like a skater at the perilous edge of ice
breathing a silent strength. Until

he places you in his domain
there is no movement of wing, talons
as rigid as old pitch around
the branch, the eyes steady as stone.

Then, only then, does he fall
into sundown, his eyes as pointed
as swords, into the stand of spruce,
into some lair, through its dark heart,

down the hollow of the windfall night.

Day on day you walk these woods
and never hear a sound. Then from
nowhere: the terrible beating of wings,
the panicked cry, the toppling home.

This domain you walk carefully in,
aware of the eyes that pierce, the hand
that fells. It is not your place to
speak, nor the place where you began,

and you will not take from the hawk
the beating wing, from the prey the one
last cry, the sun its wing of light.
Only: you count your fears here, down

down the hollow of the windfall night.

The earliest memory of the blacksmith's shop I have is one of darkness. Not blackness, but darkness, as in a cave. Even the pile of coal taking up the whole south side of the shop gave the effect of a dark, crumbling cave wall. The atmosphere was close and smelling always of the thick, sweet, sulfurous odor of burning coal. Although the large double doors to the front of the shop were usually open, there was a heavy sense of confinement, even when you were allowed to stand by the forge and turn the crank that worked the bellows to make the fire glow to an intense red, then almost white, heat. But it felt good to be there. You were always sure of that.

Perhaps it had something to do with the smith himself. His skill with the hammer and anvil was something any child took great delight in. The way he could weld metal on metal by heating and pounding was a mystery to me as deep as night itself. He was the blacksmith, and we knew him in no other way. That—now that I think of it—is the way we knew anyone in those days, by what one did day by day. It is odd today to think that *who* the smith was did not matter then; what mattered was *what* he was.

The shop was no larger than twelve by sixteen, its hardpan floor almost ceramic to the touch except where the water bin sloshed over during the periodic dunking of hot iron. It seemed larger to a six-year-old. I can remember being very frightened the first time my father took me inside the shop. A dark winter's day it was at that, the smudges on the arms and face of the smith not helping matters at all. But my fears were short-lived. I was allowed to turn the crank while my father's plow points were reddening in the mass of glowing coal. I watched as the smith then hammered away the dullness of the iron points, reshaping them into the tools that would slice through the earth of our small farm in early spring.

From that day on, I was a regular visitor to the shop. Nearly every afternoon after school, I would stop by, before walking the mile and a half home, to watch the smith at work. Once, over the course of several days, I got to see the construction of a wagon wheel. From white oak lumber, mostly two-by-fours and two-by-sixes, all the sections of the wheel except the tire were made—the hub, which was then bound by two strips of iron heat-and-hammer welded, the spokes, the rim. To have seen the final step of the construction, the shaping of the flat iron tire to a perfect welded circle, which was then fitted miraculously, perfectly, over the bracing rim that held the spokes in place, was almost like having seen the invention of the wheel; for in truth everything made in the shop was made from no plan except that which lay in the mind of the smith.

Years later I would read about the shield of Achilles and recall the wagon wheel I saw take shape in that dim place. I would tell myself that the smithy of the gods had little on the smith I knew, for he was the creator of things beyond the ordinary—the magical plow points and wheels that would never break—and his world was a Choctaw world of fire and water and darkness. Not air, not light, not beauty. But the solid world of things that would outlast all the childish dreams I knew. His was a world in the making.

Crow White

You know how crow got black, don't you? Well, it was like this. Once he was white, really white, and a master of birds and men. You know, he felt sorry for the people. They got cold in the winter. They had to eat raw fish. So crow decided to discover fire. He went to the mountain where the thunder lived. No fire. He went to the valley where the rainbow lived. No fire. I'm stupid, he said. Why didn't I think of that before? I'll go to the sun, he said. Oh, the people said, oh. I'm going, he said. And he did. Then something terrible happened. The sun must have got mad. The sky was filled with fire everywhere and burnt snowflakes drifted down. The people said, It's a miracle, that black snow. They prayed to the sun. Then they heard something. It was very weak. Caw, it said, caw. They looked over behind a bush, which had begun to burn. They were afraid. But it was only crow. He was very weak and very black. It was some tough fight, he said, but I won.

In his later years, when the smith had hung up his tongs and hammer, the shop was silent most days of the week. But on Saturdays this one and that would, with the permission of the present owners, my cousins Jack and Lola, proprietors of Curtis's Grocery, open the shop in order to shape shoes for his horse or mule. The art of horseshoeing was a vanishing art as far back as the early forties. The only way anyone learned how to shoe horses in our neck of the woods was to be at the blacksmith's shop on Saturday, the only day of the week that the smith would consent to shoe horses and mules. When the smith retired and moved away from our small community, the romance of the blacksmith's shop was gone for me. The novice Cyclopes now at the forge were

poor images of a way of life that seemed to have passed
with the smith's going. The mystery was no longer there;
the shop was little more than a dirty little hovel that had
lost its dark luster with the passing of an era.

By the end of World War II the blacksmith's shop was
closed even on Saturdays. Only rarely would you find the
doors propped open and the bellows whirling, for the few
farmers or ranchers who survived the Great Depression and
World War II were trucking their horses to Wister, twelve
miles to the northeast, for shoeing. In time the shop became
little more than another outdoor privy and shelter for stray
dogs. But somewhere in the interval, about the time I started
high school, it became a kind of clubhouse par excellence
for me and several of the boys I ran around with. We could
always hang out there without fear of our parents' intrusion.
After all, there was a massive chain and lock holding the
doors securely together, and no one but us knew of the
secret entrance, two loose boards on the blind side of the
building. We could roll our own Bull Durham cigarettes
there without fear of discovery.

The amazing thing I learned about the blacksmith's shop
was that it was not first a blacksmith's shop at all—amazing
to me as a child because I could not visualize anything
beyond the glowing forge, the coal, the massive forearms
of the smith. For a long while, after my first few visits to
the shop, I had been aware that adjacent to the one room
of the forge was another, longer, room. I found that both
rooms of the building had been used as a repair shop and
garage before World War I, when my own uncle, Jack Adams, had a service station and repair shop where he serviced
an occasional Model T Ford. The smith used the larger room
as a scrap heap for junk iron, which he was constantly sorting
through for usable materials. After the shop had closed for
good, my buddies and I discovered there was much more
to it than what we had assumed in the past.

Partially hidden among all the junk of decades were several tin cases of movie reels that, presumably, had been stored in the room before the smith had started his great junk pile. We had heard that Audie Sisk, whose ancient parents still lived directly behind the blacksmith's shop, once operated a movie house in Summerfield, way back in the early years of the Depression, before he migrated to California along with half the population of eastern Oklahoma. Why he had left the films there remained a mystery we could not fathom. We could see they were silent films from the captions on some of the frames we squinted to read. To our infinite delight we would spend long Saturdays rolling and unrolling each reel, looking at each sequence of frames on every film. It was as if we held lives of characters in our hands, as if they were our secret lives. We discovered that we could rig a flashlight so that it could be used to project a dim semblance of picture upon the wall of the room. This was better than a real movie, this was our secret thing, and we reveled in it. We were willing captives in the blacksmith's cave. It was a reality that we preferred over the mundane outside world.

Then we discovered our reality was flammable. And to my infinite sorrow, we mutilated the films by cutting long strips from them and setting fire to the strips on the darkest nights in the middle of the one street of our town for the sole purpose of watching the rapid burning of silver nitrate. I am sure some of the neighbors must have seen something amazing, fire zipping along the street for a long moment and then vanishing, before tracing the flame to its source, our pocketed matches. Our parents were told; then we were told. The remainder of the films simply disappeared, and secretly I think we were glad to have them gone. Matches had tempted us, and we had sacrificed that which was giving us lasting pleasure for that which gave us only a momentary high.

I drank my first wine in the recesses of that dark place. I brewed it there from sheep-showers, a kind of purplish clover which you ferment by adding sugar and water and letting it lie in shadows for two weeks. All that was forbidden I contemplated there—city lights, circus, sex. There I could freely imagine whatever I wanted, discuss the finer points in livid debate with my friends, and occasionally blueprint the execution of some great plan.

Then as we began to forget, the blacksmith's shop burned; and in its ashes lay my childhood and adolescence. I was finishing high school, swearing on the flysheets of annuals never to return to this jerkwater town where the only sound of life was the Sunday Baptist bell banging out of tone. But I have not left, not in mind; for the blacksmith's shop remains a retreat, a sanctuary of the mind, where I can, through images of the past, dwell in safe refuge from the threatening forces of the millennium.

Autobiography: Last Chapter

Coming in again, you know the town by boards it makes
        eyes touch, summer shirtsleeves
        worn long, heavy hats pulled down.

    Always the wind stinks.

The woman you loved summers ago sits pale as bleached
        stones, her husband mad, their house a heap of
        broken bones.

The sky lies faded denim above your cousin's store; the
        false front from another age; dogeared as a
        tinhorn's wild joker, can't reflect your past in
        its cracked eye.

You want to cry, but know the sun turns tears to salt
    before they break from lids in this desperate
    town, where the only hope is a brittle Baptist
    bell banging sometimes Sundays.

You touch the woman by your side and want to explain
    the lack of paint away, but don't: she knows you
    are running back into yourself.

It is hard to remember a time when my father liked to tell stories about his wayward youth. He cultivated silence as well as he did potatoes in his later years. I was a late child, and his reticence was well known by the time I ever noticed it. But when I was very young, I remember, he did speak about what he "used to do." Of course, that was in reference to what he did before he married my mother. I can also remember her gently scoffing at him for bringing up "that stuff."

Once or twice he spoke of working for a circus. This was always in connection with the old photos we sometimes would sort through on rainy nights before bedtime, and always in connection with one puzzling (to me) photograph, dogeared at one corner and very faded: the image of my father sitting on the bottom tip of a very large (room-sized) smiling quarter moon. As a child, I was captivated by that picture. His reply to my question was always: "That was when I worked for the circus." I never really understood until my mother explained that my father's uncle operated a photography booth and traveled about from picnic to picnic, which during the teens and the twenties was much more "civil," I was led to understand, than what our county fairs with their carnivals were today. I had seen the photograph dozens of times before he told me the picture had been taken at Goats Bluff.

From that day on, Goats Bluff has had a haunting quality about it for me. As I grew into adolescence, it was hard for me to imagine there ever being anything remotely resembling a carnival on Goats Bluff. There was something eerie about the countryside there. Though the bluff rose only some seventy or seventy-five feet above Holson Creek, there was an immense sense of height as you looked out over the water and tree tops and beyond to Blue Mountain. For me it was like standing on the top of the world. I can remember there being two or three remnants of cooking pits on the bluff near the forest service road that cut along the rim. But there was no other sign that anything had ever happened there. That may have been my first real feeling of a sense of loss. Something had happened there. My father's photograph proved it. And now there was nothing.

A short two miles from Summerfield, the bluff was a favorite object of many a Sunday hike for a few of us who chummed together. We liked to explore for caves, though we harbored a certain fear that we could not really define of the bluff caves. We must have crawled into every crack in the bluff's face before we heard the story of the ghost of Ship Rock, and then we stopped. I don't recall whether the eerie sensation began before or after we learned. I'd swear, though, it came before.

Ship Rock was our name for the barn-sized rock sitting in the middle of the Gin Hole, the body of water directly below Goats Bluff. We had even swum out to it, climbed it, and dived from it before we heard about the ghost. We had never thought to question why no one, save ourselves, ever swam below Goats Bluff.

The story surfaced when my mother and I were looking at the old pictures one winter night. I asked her about the quarter moon picture, and she told me about Ship Rock. At the picnic when my father's picture had been taken (by whom remained a mystery, though presumably his uncle) there had been many activities. Swimming had, at that time, long been a great attraction, and diving from Ship Rock. Unfortunately, this time tragedy struck.

A beautiful young woman, a "friend" of my father, as my mother told it, dived but did not surface. Nor could anyone bring her up. Many were the boulders, the cracks, the crevices, and caves beneath the surface around Ship Rock, and she simply slipped through, never to surface again. That was the last picnic held on Goats Bluff.

The Drowning

From the rock
she dived into the shadow of herself,
    and, hurling

the surface
into rainbows, her form split the mirror
    of all forms,

and some god
held her long, too long for breath once held.
    Her lover

woke slowly
into death's dream, calling as one might call
    another

at dawn to
wake into a day in which each vista, distant,
    is flooded

with first light.
She did not return, her fair form held deep
            down below.

            Her lover
moaned, endured, and still the water
            held her form.

            We could not
free her from the slow shadows that she palely
            quite became.

            Though we tried
our eyes and skill, nothing came up with our breath
            but a faint

            taste of lilies
and our curses against the play of light and shadow
            down among

            the gripping
depths that held her silent, still, and we turned
            our curses

            on ourselves,
and, as the water blazed us back odd voices, our eyes
            chiseled at

            every stone.

That was the last anything ever held on Goats Bluff, my
mother said. The ghost, the slender white form of a woman,
subsequently was seen, down through the years, on any
number of late summer or autumn nights, and always in
full moonlight, lying on top of Ship Rock.

All through the summers of our adolescent discontent, we sought her form on warm moonlit nights. But she eluded us, always. We continued to swim, even in moonlight, and eventually grew to feel she was our protectress. After all, no one else ever swam where we did.

And then one autumn night we saw her.

We were approaching the bluff from across the Gin Hole, on the low side, just having come down Coleman's Ridge, where we had been hunting possums. Late October had given us the first seasonal frost, and we had been keen on checking the big persimmon trees east of the bluff. In the early evening moonlight, the frost gave off a silvery sheen. When we broke clear of the woods, we were on the bank of the creek, directly across from the bluff and Ship Rock. From where we stood, we clearly saw what appeared to be a human form lying on top of the rock.

We grew still and silent, the four of us, Chief, Johnny, Sundance, and myself. There was a sudden taste in my mouth I can remember to this day. The taste of old pennies. How many moments we stood silent, staring, I cannot say. Then someone of us said, "It's the moonlight," or "It's the frost." And just as suddenly as we were convinced we saw her, we were convinced in our outrageously high-schoolish scientific minds that all was physical phenomenon.

And so it must have been. She vanished by the time we had taken ten steps downstream.

We never were able to see her form again, though we tried time after time, season after season. There was never the exact same moon, the exact same frost, the exact same mood for us to be in. We had seen her, we had lost her—ghost or natural phenomenon, we could never be sure.

Some forty years later I would remember all of this, simply, easily, involuntarily, because of the old photograph, even more faded, that I held in my hand. I would be able to write it, to hold it as a moment out of a time when things

were different, strange, good. What could be better than
once more seeing my father sitting in the moon smiling at
someone capturing his image on a tintype that would only
gradually fade into eternity? Or hearing my aging mother
gently scoff once more, "Oh, that old thing!"?

Elegy for the Girl Who Drowned at Goats Bluff

The sun strikes water like soft stone,
oblique and torn by surface waves.
Below, in the still place of stone,
the slow fish nuzzle through the caves

you seldom know are there at all
and rest among the drowned girl's bones.
Above, the bluff is too brittle
for a date in stone. The long day downs,

and she alone records the passing.
You think you know her now, the scream
that cracked the bluff, the siren song
that wails its way into the dream

you sometimes have. Dark water.
Darker still the night. You wait
for the water to take the sky, for
the floating moon to turn stone white

as the skin of dead fish. You know
she sees you stranger to this place,
her empty eyes wide against the night,
her empty hands, her empty face.

How dull to say I was born in 1933, the fifth child, the third son, of Austin Oscar and Bessie Vernon Adams Barnes, near the town of Summerfield, in LeFlore County, Oklahoma. Yet these facts set me firmly in time and place. My earliest memories are of house and vista: from a porch facing a lane I look up and down a road that stretched to the mountains in the south and to the river to the north. It was an infinitely long road, veeing and disappearing into the blue of Winding Stair Mountain or dropping into the river I had yet to see.

Only brief moments and images remain of the few years we lived across the field from the clump of trees that protected the mound. But the house is clear in my mind as if I left it only yesterday: two rooms, with a breezeway between them. One room had a fireplace and a space for sitting and a bed, where my mother and father slept. The other contained two beds and sundry items and boxes I no longer see with any clarity at all. I do not recall where I slept, nor where we ate. But the image of the house as viewed from outside through a child's eyes is an immense one, the structure towering gray and hollow against an autumn sky.

And the image begins to fuse with another: the house on Mountain Creek Road north of Wister. And again the image of house is clear. Now a larger, more expansive dwelling, with a long front porch and no breezeway, an enormous fireplace that I could walk into when the fire was out, a kitchen as large as a bedroom. But still the color of gray persists: many houses during that time were made from green lumber fresh from local sawmills and could not be painted with any success. Even after the lumber had aged, the rough-cut boards were usually not painted. Strange that I have no memory of sunlight for the first six years of my life. Only the gray days and the deep, black nights.

The house on Mountain Creek Road seemed as large as a castle. I remember standing underneath the edge of the front porch to get out of the rain, with Colonel, my collie, sitting beside me. We were both looking across the road to a grassy prairie pasture that swept down a sloping hill to the creek beyond, where, had it not been raining, my sisters had promised to take me swimming. Conversely, I remember standing on the high bank of the swimming hole eating pawpaws my sisters had picked from the low limbs of a tree, looking back up the prairie and across the road to our house that stood, gray on gray, immense in its place on the hill.

My Father's House

i.
Below my father's house
are many meadows,

and beyond the meadows
the pawpaw trees
line the river banks.

I am alone here
where my father's voice

drifts, a small cloud,
in a sky too gray,

in a river far too clear.

ii.
What echoes there are
are here below

my father's house
among the pawpaw trees,

the shadowing leaves.

I am alone here,
stranger to words

and worlds I'll never know;
like the fruit of these trees

I grow soft

iii.
in summer wind,
remembering the firm

time, the sound of bells
in the meadows,

the lowing herds.

The dream ongoing,
the found past,

the one shadow
I always walk in,

my father's house.

From the house on Mountain Creek to Wister must have been five or six miles. More than once, when my father was freighting lumber from a sawmill he worked for during the winter months, I would get to ride atop a wagonload of fresh-cut pine lumber all the way into town. My father and his helper would sing rowdy songs as the iron-tired wheels popped gravel along the way. They would unload the resin-oozing boards into boxcars on the Rock Island or Frisco railroad sidings and then take me to the soda fountain for a double-dip ice cream cone at the only drugstore in town, tethering the team of horses between Model A Fords and Chevrolet roadsters to the hitching rail at the front of the false-front building, remaining visages of a time that was rapidly disappearing without my even knowing that another age had been.

Strange, what you recall of days that seem to gray each into the other in a time when time seems hardly to have existed at all except now as in some long dream you see from a distant sleep. Images appear, vanish, appear again in such a fashion or frequency that these are themselves the history of the place where you were and, consequently, of what you were.

Our neighbor down the road had an ugly, jagged scar on his stomach. He never wore a shirt all summer, and the pink, deep tissue just above his navel gaped wide. He had two years before been run over by the mowing machine.

He had fallen from the seat above the single crosscutting blade as the horses bolted from a striking copperhead. In his misfortune, he was lucky to escape decapitation or amputation. Accidents of that sort were common. In a land of alternating forests and farms, sawmilling and farming accidents were frequent. Eastern Oklahoma might well be referred to as the country of nine-fingered men.

I liked Joe Baldwin. He was the same age as my sister Marveda, a few years older than I. He was so strong he could lift me with one hand and put me on his shoulder. But I was terribly afraid to look at the scar, which he insisted made him strong. It must have been the first realization I had that man was mortal, for I remember that each time I saw his scar I began to think of what it might be like to be dead.

It seemed a long time we lived in the gray houses. The third was back near Summerfield, and nearer the Fourche Maline, not far from Folsom Switch, on the Frisco. Here again the scene is much the same, the long porch high off the ground, the large fireplace, and vistas of light opening up from the house to the west and south. Here, in the house at the end of a long road from Summerfield that passed by the house of Lafe and Clio Anderson, whose daughters I tried to buy when I was four years old, and the house of Mr. and Mrs. McClain, whose first names I never knew and who seemed older than the land itself, the landscape in my memory takes on the atmosphere of a Corot painting. Always there is a dark foreground of house, forest, field, with figures going about a daily life, but in the distant background a mysterious light that gives a kind of hope you know is needed to keep everything going in the idyllic world. Whether it is the memory of dark or the memory of light that interests me most, it is hard to say. I can only view the houses now as if they were in Corot paintings, a dull gray, framed in a memory of time that is mine and mine alone.

Heartland

The houses die and will not die.
The force of walls remains. Take
the family portrait hanging oval
on the wall and, underneath it
on the chifforobe, a dish of mints.

There are houses that fall, but their
shadows stay, lightly against a summer's
dusk. And there are photographs that
show ghosts of mothers walking halls,
of fathers fiddling in moonlight.

Even in disrepair, there's a life
to the houses. The rush of wind stirs
a soul: footfalls on wood and stone,
the creak of kitchen door, the last
words of a son gone away to war.

The houses die and do not die.
There is something that will not let
a space be given solely to grass.
The aura holds, the center will
not fold, forever framed against
the graying sky, the coming night.

Autobiographical Flashback: Puma and Pokeweed

I've spoken of home before and spotted crows
older than my hair. I generalize: home
is where hard is. And know it true. The crow
is constant color: his caw can crack a stone.

You keep your crows alive as best you can:
you remember a puma and pokeweed and trees
quick with wings and wind, tell yourself the fear
you felt along your fingertips would freeze

your sanity now, if you were child again,
free to feel again leaves upon your head,
to break off shoots of poke for suppertime,
to dream the cry of a puma one time heard.

Your memory is rocked by things you have
neglected; your stoned eyes are hard with world
you are late to see. And even now you know
the facts are wrong, as random and whorled

as fingerprints on records you've tried to keep
or the circling crows that blot your inland sky.

At Folsom Switch there was, in 1939, still a general store,
the foundation of which had been made of massive old logs.
Fifty feet or so up the road, by the tracks, stood a wooden
water tower, where most of the trains, freight and passenger
alike, stopped to fill their boilers. The tank was kept filled
by a line from the river, a few scant yards away, a piston
pump, and a John Deere kerosene-powered stationary motor. There was a horse trough next to the shed over the
motor that someone kept filling at the railroad's expense. I
would sit on the broad front porch of the store and look
across the muddy road to the grave of an unknown man, a
hobo they said, who had fallen under the wheels of a Frisco
freight train when this was still Indian Territory. The grave,
like the store, was just a few yards from the tracks, under
the shade of tall pin oaks. Someone had ringed it with rocks
and painted them white. The mound of dirt within the rocks
was always bare.

On one particular rainy day, my father had tethered the
horses and wagon beneath the pin oaks to keep as much
rain off them as he could, since it was pouring down in
sheets. He draped a tarpaulin over us, and we sat there
waiting for the rain to let up so we could cross the road to
the store without getting drenched. The popping of the John
Deere motor driving the pump echoed off down the river
and into the woods. He told me that before they had the
pump the railroad men had to fill the tank from barrels
they trucked up from the ford in a wagon, a process that
continued throughout most of the day. Back in the 1890s
and then a few years before World War I, there were many
more steam locomotives on the track than now, even though
we heard at least eight or ten trains each day whistling at

the crossings. That low, mournful blast from the engines late at night was as lonesome a sound as you would ever hear in a lifetime.

It was in the years just before the war, he said, that the hobo had been run over while trying to hop an eastbound express freight, which didn't stop at Folsom Switch. He was cut in half at his belt line. This, he explained, was why the grave was so very small. Years later I would think that perhaps he had been kidding me, but at the same time I knew that my father was always a truthful man and never made jokes, nor laughed at anyone else's. The ring of painted stones meant that the grave had been simply a hole, not a traditional two-by-six. I could not look at the grave on passing from then on without a cold threat of terror biting at my heels.

Our house was not actually at the end of the road. It was just the last house accessible to automobiles. Once you crossed the Fourche Maline and headed north through the bottomlands toward Folsom Switch, the road became treacherous, almost impassable: mud in the spring and autumn and deep dried wagon ruts in the summer. Our house seemed to be on the edge of a deep forest that the river ran through, that a forbidding railroad ran through, and that a road ran through to come out on the other side at a far place called Fanshawe, where I could never go in my long child's life.

Autobiography, Chapter XIII: Ghost Train, the Dream

For years that train drove every night, and its low
     dirge of steam filled the wind with a song
     beginning way beyond my eyes.

Always far off north of home, where the bottomlands
    were heavy with two slow rivers, where the cane-
    brakes splayed away into the weeping woman's
    slough, the distant roar of fire and steel drummed
    me nightly into dream.

I was cadenced by that dark engine off the edge of
    night into the dream of a drowned son, and am
    cadenced still.

For when the wind rises nights I cannot sleep, there's
    a certain droning in the air that wakes my bones:

I see the black hulk looming through the dark, its
    drivers pounding black smoke white against the
    weeping woman's moon,

and still I am lifted from myself and wailed away over
    dark water like some other mother's son.

At the ford of the river, below our house, there were
always mussels to be found and crayfish. Once in a while,
I gathered them for my mother to cook. Crawdad tails were
then a delicacy, for eastern Oklahoma was still very Southern
in its culture. The removal of the Mississippi Choctaws to
Indian Territory in the 1830s transplanted more than the
history books give credit for. It transplanted a way of life.
Cotton growing, for example, was the main source of income

for farmers in the Depression years, as it had been for nearly a century in eastern Oklahoma. Pan-fried chicken, gravy, baked sweet potatoes, and hominy grits have graced the Sunday tables in Summerfield, though I doubt anyone eats crawdad tails anymore. The food is distinctly Southern even today.

It was here near the ford that we heard the panther scream. My sisters, my mother, and I had been looking for pokeweed late one day, just across the river. I always liked going with them and getting into the tight places under fences or among the various kinds of brambles, especially blackberry briars, to break off the fresh shoots of poke that came up early every spring. (I was cautioned severely that I should not eat the plant raw, for it was deadly poison unless it were boiled three times and the water poured off each time. After the third boiling it was drained and fried, scrambled together with eggs.) My sisters had just set me over a fence where I was to break off several shoots beyond their reach, when we heard it, a low growl at first, then rising into a frantic scream.

They yelled for me to come to the fence fast, which I surely did. I can remember them lifting me, almost throwing me, over the fence and then all of us running down the hill to the ford of the river. The scream of the big cat continued for several minutes. We had heard his sounds in the night at other times, but never thought that we would ever be so close to him in broad daylight. We did not, however, see him. We were too intent on leaving his domain as fast as our legs would go. Later, that night, we heard him again. One long cry, then silence. Mr. McClain had told us that the cat had been passing through the bottoms each spring for the last five or six years—to where, he could not say.

I would remember the cry of the panther and in a child's way associate it with evil for years to come.

On Hearing the News That Hitler Was Dead

When we heard the news that Hitler was dead,
under the porch something shook we couldn't find.
The dogs were by our sides, and all the hogs
were penned. The radio was full of Europe's end
and Berlin falling into Red Russia's hands.

The grown-ups heard it and sent us in the house
with the dogs, their bristles tough as quills.
Something big bumped against the floor and made
the blackest sounds we'd ever heard. Then, still
scraping underneath, it roared aloud until

we turned as white as chalk and someone fired
a shotgun into the dark beneath the floor.
We heard hell break from down below and burst
through the front-yard picket fence: a panther
black as sin itself. They said it cleared a car

in one long leap and the ditch we couldn't jump.
We sighed and turned our normal brown as if
some threat of evil had missed us in the night.
The commentator's words on Hitler's death left
us puzzled about the course of war. A gift

of light was what we children waited for.
In the falling night we heard the far-off yowl
of wildcats in the woods, or thought we did.
The news leapt into the dark, wondering how
the master race so-called could master now

with Der Führer dead and the Russians drunk
on German schnapps. But what if he were not
the ashes they said were his? someone asked.
Silence and sound grew thick. Outside, lamplight
stumbled and fell into a starless night.

We moved to within a quarter mile of Summerfield perhaps a year before Pearl Harbor. The gray boxed house (no studs in the walls) stood on the road running west to Summerfield and east to Lone Pine. Within months of the move, my brother, Hack, had joined the Civil Conservation Corps before finishing high school, and both my sisters, Erma and Marveda, had married boys who had volunteered for military service. (Another brother, Kenneth, who was born two years before me, died in infancy from what most likely had been SIDS, though they did not call it that in the 1930s.) Times were hard for us then. My father did tenant farming for a cousin, and there was little income even when Hack, Erma, and Marveda were home to help. I had just started school and was of little use on the farm. It was here, in this house, that we heard the news of the bombing of Pearl Harbor. Hack went directly from the CCC into the Army Air Corps, and we would not see him until he returned from England four years later, after the war.

The day we heard the news on the battery radio it was cold and wet. I can almost still hear the sound of the rain on the tin roof of the house, rain that could have easily been snow if the temperature had dropped. My mother cried most of the day, and my father walked to town to talk with others about what was happening in the world. There are for me only the gray house, the gray day, the rain, and the endless news and static on the radio. I have no memory of leaving the house on the day Pearl Harbor was bombed.

In a short time, most of the young men were enlisted, either by draft or through volunteering. Tiny white flags started appearing in the front windows of houses along the roads. Each had a blue star or stars upon it, depending on how many sons and daughters were away at war. I felt alone and was very much alone during the war years. I *was* an only child essentially. Always after school and during the summers, I was left entirely to my own devices, and they were various.

In relation to the war, I was hawkish. Everyone in eastern Oklahoma was a hawk. To have been a dove would have meant you would have been called a Jap lover or Kraut lover. The games I played were war games. When others were crazy for basketball, I was fighting on all fronts, imagining the way it was over there. I was aviator, infantryman, submariner: I did it all over and over again. If children could have gone to war, I would have enlisted immediately. Even my dreams were full of war, and I do not apologize for that.

The Sawdust War

On the early summer days I lay with back
against the sawdust pile and felt the heat
of a thousand pines, oaks, elms, sycamores
flowing into my flesh, my nose alive
with that peculiar smell of death the trees
became. Odd to me then how the summer rain
made the heat even more intense. Digging
down the dust, I began to reshape a world

I hardly knew: the crumbly terrain became
theaters of the war. I was barely ten.

What I knew of the wide world and real war
came down the valley's road or flew over
the mountains I was caught between. Remote
I was nightly glued to the radio,
wondering at reports of a North African
campaign and Europe falling into chaos.
All daylight long I imitated what I
thought I heard, molding sawdust into hills,
roads, rivers, displacing troops of toys,
claiming ground by avalanche and mortar

fire, advancing bravely into black cities,
shrouding the fallen heroes with white bark.
I gained good ground against the Axis through
long summer days. Then one morning, dressed in
drab for hard work of war, I saw real smoke
rising from my battlefield. Crawling from
beneath the sawdust like vague spiderwebs,
claiming first the underground, then foxholes,
it spread like a wave of poison gas across
the woody hills I shaped with a mason's trowel.

I could not see the fire: it climbed from deep
within. No matter how I dug or shifted dust,
I could not find the source. My captured ground
nightly sank into itself. The gray smoke
hovered like owls under the slow stillness
of stars, until one night I woke to see,
at the center, a circle of smoldering sparks
turning to flame, ash spreading outward and down.

All night the pile glowed red, and I grew ashamed
for some fierce reason I could not then name.

   I was a child, and in a child's way I saw the war as an
adventure, a way out of the dull life that I thought I knew
too well. My fantasies of war were as broad as nights were
long, filled with deeds others had done, according to Captain
Midnight and Sky King on the radio or Captain Easy and
Joe Palooka in the comic strips.

Written during the Funeral of Hirohito

Earthbound they stood as monuments to air,
warplanes all rowed with their teeth to the wind
that thundered in from the lightning west. Mystery
covered them, black and drab hiding scars from
flak and cannon fire. Those beings from a sky
I did not know held me. Lights of the fair

flashed bare bulbs down the midway, and barkers
spieled sucker lines in megaphones. From my stance
beneath the tatooed nose of a Black Widow,
I saw the night slide over us, clouds and dim
stars inbound from the Pacific. In the far
hills west, a high roll of drums and faster

light. I remember rain, the splatter of large
drops on wings and tails, tents filled with air.
The planes off-limits, I snailed up a narrow
ladder propped against the cold cockpit
to lean heavenward on the clear canopy
of glass and feel the storm wind descend hard

to lift us off the world. All the world known
to me stretched off into the night below.
In a fantasy of war, I flew missions
no man could fly and returned shattered to do
again that which could not be done. I lived
in minutes a life I would not give the gone

years for. The tumult of the county fair rolled
under the night fighter's blackened wings. Held
clouds bursting into terrifying light,
the storm surrounded us. Parents ran for
cars, and children scampered through exhibits.
I was ten then and knew I had control.

In this the last house of my childhood, I would discover
another world beyond radio and comic strips. The world of
reading opened before me, a flowering dawn that I walked
into almost daily from the time I started to grade school. I
devoured every book I could get my hands on. And with
time on my hands, I read nightly until my father forced me
to bed with a reminder that kerosene for lamps was scarce
and ten cents a gallon. It is reading, nothing else, that ultimately made me want to write. Nothing in the blood or the
genes or the culture of eastern Oklahoma made me want to
become a writer. I fell in love with the art of writing twenty
years before I knew what had afflicted me. It would take
two more wars and a decade in the Pacific Northwest and
at least a thousand volumes of reading before I would be
ready to write one word.

A quarter mile north of the Gin Hole lies a hundred-yard stretch of water that we used to call the Sand Bar, because of an abundance of sand collected on the south bank in flood time by swirling eddies as Holson Creek rushed down the shoals between Goats Bluff and the Sand Bar. There was a natural spring at the edge of the sandy bank, flowing out from under the sycamores, that we delighted in drinking from. On the unbearably hot days of summer, we would lie in the pool formed by the spring and feel the lift of cool, clear water transport us into an idyllic land free from the muggy heat of the Oklahoma August.

Of the summer choices we had in the years of discontent that was our adolescence, the one foremost in mind was always to spend the day at the Sand Bar swimming and lying in the sun, while the clouds and birds coursed overhead and our world was free of daily lumber. Nothing mattered in our world when we were there, Chief and me. It was we who kept the diving board wedged between two huge water willows in good repair, replacing the supports when they rotted and making sure the Tarzan swing just beyond the board was adjusted at the right length for catapulting us into the middle of the deep pool.

The Sand Bar: it was a wonder to us that it existed at all. On the whole twenty-mile length of the stony banks of Holson Creek, it was the only place where sand collected in any significant proportion. You could haul away tons of sand without its being missed. It was an oasis, an island in a jungle of green.

There was a sense of wilderness about Holson Creek (a short river, actually, and fierce in flood). No houses lined it, and none were visible as you walked its banks or broke through its tangled woods and canebrakes. Cottonmouths, copperheads, rattlesnakes could be seen nearly any day, and we had to be careful as we walked. But at that point in time we were experienced woodsmen: we knew how to be in relation to terrain.

By the time I was twelve we could spend days in the woods and along the stream and in the hills above it without going home for food. Game was plentiful, especially *funi* (squirrels) and *chukfi luma* (rabbits), and I was a crack shot with a .22 rifle.

Rabbits

A single-shot .22
and steady hand
could make you king
among the beasts
or ashamed to face
the checker players
who were too old
to beat the field.

You killed because
you loved it
still; they crowned

kings reluctantly,
spat between cracks.

You could not know
the checkerboard
held acres
and each move
was deadly as
a hollowpoint.

You shot rabbits
until you lifted
the last one by the ears
and found a brain
checked, crossed
with a thousand moves
a rabbit had to take.

We knew where the big bass fed, and what berries and
other vegetation we could safely eat. With the help of the
MacGowen boys, Johnny and Hughie, we had built lean-to
cabins at the Sand Bar, at the mouth of Holson Creek, and
on Nanny Ridge to the west of old Hosey's apple tree, each
"hideout" about two miles distant from the other, and from
each cabin we would radiate out to explore the unknown
country beyond. Though I seldom spent the night in the
deep woods, often I would be there from dawn to full dark
before going home, dead tired but full of the feeling that
I had spent the day the way I would like the world to
forever be.

One Sunday in early May when I was twelve, the four of
us set out from the crude lean-to cabin that we had built on
Nanny Ridge, heading for the blue valley we could see from
our lookout, a tall post oak. We thought the blue valley was

Tom Fry Hollow, which we had been told held the ruins of a ranch house that dated back at least a hundred years. We were, with the warmth of spring upon us, anxious to explore. The walk through underbrush up and down the ridges was pure adventure to us, and in an hour's time we broke out onto the flat floor of the small valley. In the distance, toward the south, we could see horses grazing. At a time when most of the mountains that make up the northwestern slopes of the Ouachita National Forest were free range, it was strange to see horses free of fetters or fence. Wild horses, we exclaimed, but knew that that could not be.

For most of the afternoon we frolicked like colts in the prairie grass. Toward sundown we found ourselves at the south edge of the valley, where the homestead had been. There were remnants of the house scattered about: a few rotting logs, a window frame with rusted square nails protruding, some unidentifiable scraps of metal. The house seemed to have simply rotted away over the long course of years. No one had lived in Tom Fry Hollow for a hundred years from the looks of things now. As the sun dropped to the valley's head, we decided to look for the horses, who were nowhere in sight. We tried to find tracks, but the ground was too dry and the grass too thick. We heard a whinny back in the line of trees but could distinguish nothing in the coming shadows.

The ghosts of those horses haunt me still. I often wonder whose they were and why they were there. No one in that part of the country let horses onto free range. For horses had a tendency to wander for miles and miles beyond home ground, whereas cattle and pigs kept relatively close to the farms and ranches. Perhaps we had just imagined there were horses in Tom Fry Hollow. It was after all a fabulous place, a place that no one had told us about, a serene and peaceful valley that was ours to discover on our own.

Scouting Tom Fry Hollow

The trail I blazed on pine is gone
without a trace. The lay of the land and sky
has run amuck. I check the ridge south,
look for marks I know cannot be there now.

One thing remains unchanged. The hollow hard
below: the brown, brown grass flowing around
chimney rubble and collapsed corral, the sound
of distant wolves keening in the stony hills.

I go down, as before, to look for the grave
I will not find again. The wind always
blows and sundown comes hours ahead of time.
Little chance any artifact is left

to clear the name of bones the hollow bears.
Grave unmarked, the hanged man still hangs under
the ghost of every tree. I raise a stone,
poor homage, for the next man to wonder on.

The first summer after Pearl Harbor had been attacked—I was seven—was especially hard for us, as I recall. My father had not been able to get the fertilizer he needed in the spring for his cotton and had had to plant without it. Then there was too much early rain, and later too much sun. As we chopped away, thinning the cotton to two stalks for each length of a hoe blade, he said there wasn't much need. The plants would yield very little. And indeed, he barely realized a bale for all of his labor. The following summers were but a little better if at all.

I don't know how we survived the lean war years. My mother had hoarded ration stamps so she would not have enough to buy sugar to make blackberry jelly with when the berries matured in June. The taste of sugar was a rare treat for me in those days. We did, however, have a garden, and it saved us from falling over the brink of starvation. The garden often proved to be a means by which we could trade for staples and for me a means by which I could gain admittance to the tent show that came every summer for two weeks during the course of the war. But when there were no green onions to trade for tickets to the movies, I along with a half dozen other boys would slip in under the tent as soon as the lights went out.

The last summer of the war—I was still in grade school—
I remember most clearly. There was absolutely nothing for
us to do in Summerfield. Since cotton had failed so badly,
no one was now farming enough to need help in the fields.
There was no money to be earned. We had just the dull
passage of slow, hot days on our backs as we lay on the
river banks. Then the tent show came back to town, and
daily we were there looking at the posters and stills before
the dark flap of the tent.

There is an image I carry with me to this day from some
tragic movie we saw that summer: a dark forest, a steep
road rounding a moonlit lake, and a dog coming up from
the lake through the ghostly trees to the road carrying a
man's shoe. I remember nothing of the film except that
image, and threads of a song far in the background that
was night:

> love, O love, O careless love,
> you took my heart and now you're gone,
> love, O love, O careless love,

sung by Tex Ritter or some other singing cowboy. A strong
sense of loss touches me each time the image comes. Strange,
to be haunted by such insignificant things.

Each night the tent show was in Summerfield, there must
have been at least a half dozen of us boys who rolled under
the tent because we didn't have the money to buy tickets.
I don't know which was the greatest pleasure: the thrill of
seeing a good movie or the thrill of slipping in under the
tent. Once or twice a tentwalker would catch one of us by
the heel, but it really didn't matter. In a few minutes' time
we would again be at the edge of the tent. I think the movie
man expected a good number of his moviegoers to be children of the night.

The movies I saw helped sustain me. In a dreary time when life on the home front was slow and dull, I needed the adventures of heroes to carry me into some other world, a world where you could be another. Without reading and the movies, I would have gone mad in a crazy world of childhood. Across the pages I followed the action of many a man and woman. Westerns, detective stories, romance novels—I read everything impartially. But it was on the silver screen that I lost myself entirely. In watching movies I became what I could not be. I was Colonel Tim McCoy (a bona fide World War I decorated hero), Gene Autry (who'd once been a telegrapher on the Frisco line), Bob Steele (whose lightning fists were never still), Johnny Weismuller (whose German name was never questioned), and a multitude of others, even once in a while a "good" Indian, strong and tall, standing my ground against evil. And once in a while, as the long summers passed, I realized, with the better movies, few though they were, that there were forces of evil loosed on the world I had little knowledge of.

Under the Tent

The traveling show stretched its canvas
over the bluegrass behind the store
when we were ten, the last picture
shows we'd get to see during the war

the Axis forced on us. We crouched
by the flapping tent. The summer wind
at night was mischief in our heads,
blowing wild thyme in our hair. Then

we were full of war, those of us
too young to go. We claimed to know
all battlegrounds through hell and back.
What we wanted to do was throw

enough of the dark upon our skins
to slip beneath all tents unseen,
as the night patrol did in the film
we saw that summer before the end.

We had to time it right: to roll
exactly under the tent the way
you roll away from quick danger
in your sleep. Or we'd have to play

the fool when the tentwalker caught
us by the neck. Our detailed plan
precise, we penetrated the held
blackness the exact moment when

the light went out and the silver
screen lit up, rolling in unison
into farmers' heavy legs, spittle,
sleeping dogs, climbing into sound

and light, an illumination
we understood more than the real.
Such ecstasy of risk carried us
into ourselves and into the world.

In 1942 we moved ten miles south of Summerfield, to Holson Valley, a narrow depression between the foothills of Winding Stair Mountain to the south and the ridges of Blue Mountain to the north. For the remainder of the war we would live here, near the headwaters of Holson Creek. My father was still trying to grow cotton on shares for an absentee landlord and trying to get a small herd of cattle started from the few head of Herefords he had managed to hang on to—both without much success, but game was a little more plentiful in the mountains and the creek provided a source for good channel catfish. So we were not as hungry as we had been in the house nearer Summerfield.

It was during this time that I knew I was no longer a child: I could stand my ground with a rattlesnake and I could hear the yap and yowl of wolves without fear. From the time I was eight through eleven, I roamed the woods and streams of Holson Valley and in the company of friends began to learn to be at one with the land. Later, when we once again moved back to the Summerfield region, I would be well prepared to scout the bottomlands from the confluence of Holson Creek and Fourche Maline to hills beyond Nanny Ridge and Tom Fry Hollow.

Sundays after church my close buddies and I would take off for the woods or the creek immediately after having Sunday dinner (lunch, in the vernacular) with the folks. One Sunday Manny, my cousin, and Billy Blankenship and I set out for the bluff above Cedar Creek, a tributary of Holson, just south of Billy's house, to explore. In our bumbling way we stumbled onto a den of rattlers that smelled of a deadly venom. Ordinarily we would have told our fathers, but for some reason we kept the knowledge to ourselves. Not even after Deck Wylie had been bitten did we tell anyone where the crevice of snakes was situated.

It was not, however, without a sense of guilt that I went with Nanny and Billy to see old Deck's black leg. Deck and his brother Toad had been cutting pulpwood up the northern slopes of Winding Stair Mountain, not far from where we had found the rattlesnake den, when he had stepped on the rattlesnake and was bitten between the knee and ankle of his left leg. Foolishly, they had taken the time to run down and kill the six-foot rattlesnake before Toad had driven Deck the fifteen miles to Talihina in the logging truck for treatment at the Indian hospital. By the time they reached the hospital, the leg all the way to the hip had swollen twice its normal size. It was a miracle he survived, they said. He had been hot and sweaty when the snake struck him, and he had not cooled off at all in the killing of the snake. He vomited greenish bile for two days, and the leg turned black as a stovepipe.

Deck was lying on a sofa when we stepped through the door. He waved us over and lay back a fold of his pants leg, which had been ripped open to accommodate the swollen mass. The leg glistened in its tight blackness. The smell was awful, exactly what we had smelled when we had discovered the den. A wave of nausea rolled over me as we bolted for the door. All I could think was that he was going to die. He smelled like dying, and that was that. We swore

an oath that we would never tell what we knew because
they would accuse us of murder. We saw snakes where no
snakes were for the rest of the day.

Deck managed, somehow, to survive the poison and carried the ten-point rattle as a charm against being bitten
again. The leg gradually assumed its normal appearance,
except for a half dozen two-inch scars from the cuts Toad
had made on it to let the poison out after they had killed
the snake. In my worse dreams I saw us all bitten and black
and dead. But within a year I could stand still while a rattler
crossed the road. I knew what he was capable of and how
to avoid him so that what fear I had had was a fear that
taught me to live among such crawling things.

Touching the Rattlesnake

The neighbor's leg was black from toe to thigh,
with yellow pus oozing from cuts he'd made
trying to stop the poison from reaching
his heart. He showed the three of us stumbling
into his house, after Sunday school set
us free, what he said we would be afraid
to see. The swollen blackness made me shudder
with adolescent sins I knew we were doomed
to hell for. He dared us to touch the leg.

Tight as the shell of a dried gourd, the skin
seemed to break with each slight movement he made.
I left with the smell of venom in my lungs,
my eyes careful with every rock we passed
on the way to the swimming hole. I lay
on the shoal and felt the current crawl along
my body until all thoughts of fangs were washed
away and the rattle of leaves above my head
seemed only leaves. *Amazing grace, how sweet*

I sang straight up into the Sunday sky.
The others splashed my face, and we wallowed
like carp in the mud. We could not know that one
of us would die before the sun went down, fangs
buried in his neck as he reached over a boulder
to pull himself up the face of the cliff above
the swimming hole. Nor that he would live just
long enough to climb back down, boasting that
he touched the snake before it struck his neck.

The neighbor did not die, but thrived on guts
he said it took to have a snaky leg.
I could not forget the oozing blackness
and never crossed his door again, nor how
white the naked body of my friend lay.
The wind rose late that day and made the limbs
crash above our heads. That night it rained.
The sound of thunder and shotguns carried us
through a domain of snakes we would annihilate.

It was a dangerous country for anyone who dropped his
guard. Snakebite was not at all uncommon in the years
before and during World War II. Isaac Self, whose father
had operated a portable sawmill in the region a few years
before Deck was bitten, had reached down to fasten a choker
around a log he was skidding to a loading dock and had
been bitten by a diamondback rattler. He had slit a gash on
his right forefinger between the first and second knuckles
and sucked blood and venom from the finger for two hours
and drunk a half quart of rotgut whiskey. He survived without medical treatment, but the finger was as stiff as a board
for the rest of his life.

I don't remember ever walking the dirt roads of Holson
Valley without seeing tracks where snakes had crossed. One

day Uncle Bob Blankenship, Billy's grandfather, picked a cottonmouth up by the tail, after holding the head with his crooked hickory walking cane, and cracked it like a whip until the back of the snake snapped. It writhed with a broken spine until he beat its head to a pulp with the end of his cane. No one really cared about the balance of nature or protecting the environment in those days—at least not as much as about making one's own personal domain safe from the "forces of nature"—an attitude we realize wrong far too late. The fear of snakes was real in Holson Valley, and the fear was well founded. There is little doubt about that.

More than anything else, however, the overgrazing of cattle and destructive rooting of hogs on the free range of the national forest, which ran parallel to both sides of Holson Valley in the forties and fifties, thinned the poisonous snake population down nearly to the point of annihilation. Hogs, especially, were a threat to snakes. Seldom did hogs even get sick from a snake bite, and they would eat the snake if they could get to it. Snakes and acorns were, in effect, good feed for fattening hogs.

There was something of a haunted atmosphere about Deadman's Trail and the small, secluded valley through which it ran. The trail was wide and visible where it broke off from the Holson Valley road and headed directly up a branch valley toward the Kyrkendahl ranch. I never had the desire to walk very far up Deadman's Trail or even the narrow one-mile valley it coursed to the foot of the mountain. Beyond the Kyrkendahl's place, the trail began to grow less visible as it curved into the hollows at the base of Winding Stair Mountain, which in local relief seemed to tower like Alps I had seen in encyclopedias.

As the trail started up the lower slope of the mountain, just beyond the prairie that was the site of the Kyrkendahl ranch (house, barn, and corncrib), it also began a steep and zigzagging two-mile ascent. There was something about walking the trail, a certain air of mystery that seemed to surround you at times, a kind of deep loneliness that you could almost give a name to. In the valley below the mountain the prairie teemed with wildlife. Deer, foxes, and wolves knew it as hunting grounds, and I know it must have been a favorite camping place for native clans long before Judge Holson and the Choctaws settled in the larger Holson Valley in the mid-1800s. As a child I saw it as a storybook place, with its wildlife and alpine landscape, its picturesque beauty. But neither Manny, Billie, nor I ever let the sun set on us before we left Deadman's Trail and the small valley it ran through.

No one could tell us exactly which dead man was buried on the trail: his identity had long past faded out of memory. We knew only that the trail was active before the military cut the road across the mountains from Summerfield to Talihina and on to Antlers in the days immediately following the arrival of the Choctaws. The trail ended on top of Winding Stair Mountain at a large ever-flowing spring, which even now is called Horse Thief Springs. All evidence of the trail's continuing on down the other side of the mountain has been obliterated by the forces of time, though one has to assume that it did descend into the expansive Kiamichi Valley and perhaps beyond to Texas, a hard day's ride. The fact is that in the 1940s the trail was no longer needed by anyone, for the Forest Service had cut a narrow road to the top of the mountain from the Holson Valley Road about a mile to the west of Deadman's Trail.

The trail is faint today, but in certain places you can still see where hoofs have cut into the earth and left a lasting defile across two or three branches that cascade down the steep slopes of the mountain. I cannot stand for a moment on or near the trail without a sense of a presence about me. Ghosts of all that have been part of the trail seem to gather to tell me I am not alone. And I know, in brief moments such as this, that I am shaped by the environment of my early years, by the landscape, and by the stories that come down to us through the ages that we can know only through keeping the telling alive.

There is a recurring urge for me to name the dead man whose grave names the trail, but I know I never will. The haunting atmosphere of the valley stirs in me an obligation to speak of the valley, the trail, the mountain beyond, the people who passed that way. So I remember, faintly at first, then more vividly as the years fall away and the grass is taller, the sky grayer, the mountain more distant yet looming as a great blue-black entity no one could ever reckon with. There are stories here that bend the imagination. It is sad to think you can never tell them right. But you must keep on trying.

Going up Deadman's Trail

The failure of stone
beneath your feet
is constant, cracked chert
white as bleached bone.

The trail ascends
a mountain you alone
want to wander on.
A crow, high, begins

a song. You note numbers
on a stone, cracks across
its face. Moss
blurs

the name you wouldn't
know in years.
The crow's caw sears
the open wound

you initial on the high,
runed grave.
The crow begins to rave:
he tries

a higher pitch,
one you half believe,
something with live
and die in it, with

words you don't like
to hear. Again you start
to climb. You mark
the trail, the day, the life.

Though try we did, as children will with others of their
own generation, to find out about the grave on Deadman's
Trail, we never found out anything except that there was
a grave near the foot of the mountain. Suicide, hanging,
ambush—we considered the possibilities. Nobody we ever
heard of killed themselves for love, fame, or money. No
knowledge of hanging or ambush was passed on to our generation.

The day of the horse thief was gone forever. Only the
mystery remained, and the feeling that something more was
there to be known. So the mind was free to shape its stories,
to build on the memory of what was or what could have
been. We never knew the questions to ask of our elders.
Even if we had known what to ask in relation to what was
or had been, I doubt that we would have. Those of us who
were the children of the 1930s and early 1940s in eastern
Oklahoma were and are of a different breed, I like to think:
we did not question our elders about the brutal facts of
life. We may have stood in awe and learned, but we never
questioned. We listened when the grown-ups spoke. We
valued their words, which were given freely but never
wasted. Our small imaginations thrived on language and
landscape. We invented and imagined lives. We had the
freedom and the nearly limitless leisure to live inventive

lives. Without those early years and the places I lived them
in, I would have no art.

Rest Stop at Horse Thief Spring

The air is thin enough to make you cry
for home, and sounds among the cracking stones
ring of rattlers and long-dead horses' bones.
The military crossed here first, then horse
thieves walled the spring and stayed to build

a stone corral and die. A grave is opened
every year and all stones turned up for gold.
The laughter of dead mouths is keening in
the wind. Like waves, the thud of hoof on stone
never dies. A crow is drinking from the spring.

Three thousand feet above the valley's floor,
you caw the carnivore away and taste
his wild flight in water as old as sin
and cold as nights under this winter sky.
You hear the horses' breath, their frantic leap,
their rage to know the prairie far below.

Let them turn stones. Or tourists piss
in springs. Miles away from woman and sleep,
you know this sky is full, this earth alive
with sounds it will take you long days to hear.
You give five minutes more: to dream an ambush
and a hanging as heavy as this mountain's back.

There are three things I recall about the Kyrkendahl ranch.
One is that Deadman's Trail passed right by the front door.
Another is that Elmo Kyrkendahl must have weighed over

three hundred pounds. And another is that Elmo had a dozen horses that he seldom rode, though his mother, a widow, rode almost daily in tending the horses and cattle. One Sunday, Manny, Billy, Billy's brother Robert, and I were visiting Elmo. He was far too heavy. Even we knew that. And he was older than us by a couple of years. He would lumber along like a great bear each day down the trail to Holson Valley Road to catch the schoolbus. During the summer he seldom left the shade of his front porch despite the urgings of his concerned mother. Elmo liked to read. In fact, that is all he wanted to do. He had a large and wonderful collection of Big/Little Books, most of which had at the top right-hand corner of each page a one-inch framed picture. When flipped rapidly by thumb, these frames would set in motion a story of some living magnitude. I loved the Big/ Little Books, especially the Red Ryder series, with Red and Little Arrow stumbling onto and through their many adventures of ranchland life.

It was summer, and after a large Sunday dinner Elmo wanted only to sit on the porch and thumb the corners of Captain Marvel with a faraway look in his eyes. He had given each of us a book for the afternoon's enjoyment, but he wanted it understood that we were not to take them home. Elmo's mother came to the door from the kitchen and asked Elmo if he would go fetch Bayboy so she could ride over to visit with Manny's mother for the rest of the afternoon.

Elmo moved slowly but seemed to know where the horse was, and with an ear of corn in one hand and bridle in the other he found it a quarter mile from the house at the point where the mountain seemed to lift sharply upward. A hundred yards away we saw a small mound and two large native stones standing upright in the earth. "That's the grave," he said. Then he proceeded to spook us with a story about

lights late at night and a terrible moaning on the wind when
the autumn rains begin to fall. By the time we walked back
to the ranch house, sticking very close to Elmo and Bayboy,
our faces were drained of color and Robert had begun to
cry out from sheer fright. Then we ran all the way to the
Blankenship house, with Robert wailing behind us. Elmo
knew how to tell a story, or how to frighten kids, which
sometimes amounts to the same thing.

The Ranch, Wild Horse Canyon, 1943

The mountain south of the ranch leaned hard through
a heavy sky almost blocking the winter sun
at noon. The canyon ended there, dammed by the blue
haze that Winding Stair became after a winter rain
or snow. You could hear all the horses neigh at you

from the timbered slopes on clear December nights
when the wind was down. Stars were always on the move
across the narrow patch of sky. Lying just right
in your bunk by the window, you saw ridges shove
all the higher constellations across the night

and thought of all the things you'd like to do before
your light went out and your small voice was stilled. At ten
you were wise enough to want a few summers more
to ride the ranch with the hired hands, to pretend
no end of things. But things began to end. The roar

of warplanes overhead each day made the air dance
and the canyon echo with the drumming of stampede.
The rancher's elder son joined up, finding a chance
in war to leave for a wider world. You felt a need
to keep the horses free and cried to see them prance

into the boxcars, into soap and glue, to save
the world. Days were full of planes and nights of solemn
radio, commentators mournful and slow, wave after wave
of static as the battery wore down. You were dumb
with grief at the loss of horses, dumb with ways

to call them home, yet old enough to know the dead
horses would not neigh again under the mountain moon.
You wept as a child at the stockyard gate, your knees red
with earth, and swore in time to come horses would run
free as far as the mountain's end and the canyon's head.

Uncle Bob Blankenship was an ancient man, but he could whittle the keenest sword and slimmest dagger you ever saw from the white pine slats of Washington State apple crates. All the children of Holson Valley loved that man, the killer of snakes and the teller of tall tales that set your mind adrift in a world of wonder. Strange, what you remember after a lifetime of forgetting. I remember his killing the snake. I remember his whittling me a long sword out of an apple crate. I remember riding in the back of a truck across the Beaver Pond, on the upper reaches of Holson Creek, and up the side of Blue Mountain, which was the northern boundary of Holson Valley, to within a few hundred yards of the Blue Mountain forestry lookout tower—riding up to Uncle Bob's house, where the valley people had gathered for his wake. I do not remember him dying, nor do I remember him ill. He was a lively and ancient man who knew the ways of the land and the needs of children, knew them far better than any of our parents did. He was as old as the earth itself, and every time I go back to the valley I can still see him walking down the long valley road, a cane in one hand and the hand of a child in the other.

He used to visit us when we lived near the Fourche Maline, riding the schoolbus the ten miles from Holson Valley, then walking the rest of the way from Summerfield. He would tell my mother and father he wasn't going back up the creek until they agreed to take him and spend a couple of days there. My father would harness his team of horses to the iron-tired wagon and we would set out early in the morning for the all-day drive up Holson Creek. In my memory, the trips we made up Holson Creek by wagon have run together. The several times we must have gone stand out vividly as one wonderful day's drive, although I am sure that each time we went I must have slept much of the way. Nevertheless, even before we moved into Holson Valley I knew all the landmarks along the way—Nanny Ridge, Goats Bluff, the two fords that had to be crossed on the creek, Tightwad Hill and the rotting schoolhouse there, the side roads, and where the Turners lived, the Earls, the Howertons, the Wylies, the Barneses, the Blankenships.

My world was enriched by that ancient man. His stories were of old times, a time I could hardly even imagine. He was probably eighty years of age when we moved onto the Chase Ranch in the valley (my father sharecropped there for a year before striking out on his own and gradually over the years acquiring a small herd of mixed-breed Herefords). He always had a story to tell. He had lived in the valley all his life and could chronicle human endeavor as far back as the Civil War. He told us of great deer hunts on the Arkansas River to the northwest, in Arkansas. He spoke of times when tribal councils were held on Judge Holson's ranch at the head of Holson Valley. He told us of the lost gold mines of the Choctaws and the thirteen men who took its secret with them to their graves. (He said that he himself had found quartz bearing traces of gold up Wild Horse Canyon.) Though I do not recall him saying anything about Deadman's Trail, I am convinced that he knew more stories about and more history of Holson Valley and the mountains called

Blue and Winding Stair than anyone who had ever lived
there.

Halcyon Days

Charlie Wolf used to whittle skinning knives
and swords from empty apple crates in winter.
He carved out blades I knew would never break,
true blades I knew instead would slice right through

any weed I chose to make a running deer
or any Rhode Island Red I chose to see
as enemy of God and man. Each old hen
knew my whoop meant feathers lost or worse

and squawked accordingly. Old Charlie used
to say that's why we got so many eggs
double-yoked—"scared the stuff right out of them
with that sword and that wild-eyed Choctaw yell."

Every sword I ever had before Charlie
drowned drunk on a coon hunt on the Arkansas
smelled of apples. Streaking round the barnyard
junk like a bullsnake after chicks, I breathed
pure Christmas before each ambush of red hens,
the white pine sword gleaming between my teeth.

The sounds of cowbells are surely the first sounds I remember hearing. There is something sad about the distant sound of a cowbell ringing off in the twilight as the slow cows come home for milking. This association of cowbells and sundown with sadness probably comes from those years we lived on the Chase Ranch when so many men we knew or knew of were lost at war. *Killed in battle, lost at sea, missing in action* were terms that became commonplace in our lives. We lived with a deepening sense of loss and fear for my brother, Haskell, and my brothers-in-law, Athel Billings and Chester Hamner, and their close encounters with death.

Surrounded by the atmosphere of fear and loss, we tried daily to live a normal life, to do the things we had to do to keep well and sane. My father farmed, still trying to raise enough cotton to see us through lean years, and tended the Chase cattle and the few of his own. My mother raised a garden whenever she could, and we always gathered blackberries and huckleberries in the summer. Lined on the foreheads of my parents was that feeling made visible: even these few simple things could be taken away at any time. Young as I was, I knew that fate and the world at war cared not a whit for what we suffered.

It was in the midst of this that Sonny disappeared one day in late summer. He was barely four years old. He and his sister, Sue, still in diapers, were staying with us while my sister Erma worked at the state's tuberculosis hospital in Talihina. I remember it was late in the day when we missed him. My father, mother, and I raced about the yard, the barnyard, the hill beyond the house. There was no sign of him anywhere. Then my father saw faint tracks leading down the hill just west of the woodpile. Farther down the hill the tracks became plain in the dust of the cattle trail to the deep hole of water, on Holson Creek, three hundred yards north of the house. I can still feel the rush of fear sweeping over me. We ran to the darkening stream. Not a ripple showed anywhere on the surface. The sun and wind were down. Night was near. I could hear the sound of cowbells coming up the meadow. In my mind's eye I saw him drowned, just beneath the surface near the bank where a cold spring flowed into the stream.

But his tracks led to the west along the cattle trail, through a white clay gulley that must have looked like a canyon to him. We saw where he had unerringly made his way up its side to continue his now beeline westerling down the wider trail that was once the railroad track of Dierks Lumber Company at the turn of the century. Now nothing was left of the track, not even a tie, except an occasional spike rusted red in the mountain dirt. The railhead had been at the western end of Blue Mountain. The narrow-gauged railroad had hauled lumber from the camp to the kilns at Heavener, some fifteen torturous miles to the east. I had trouble believing the railroad ever existed, though the proof was there. I was saddened to think that things pass away. And now there was Sonny, missing. But by this time my father felt certain he knew where Sonny was headed.

Melvin and Maudy Barnes (Manny's father and mother and my father's first cousins) lived just beyond the point

where the trail joined the Holson Valley Road. We could
see the big yellow schoolbus sitting in front of the house
(the fall term at LeFlore had begun in early August). Sonny
had loved riding the schoolbus and chattered about it nearly
all the time, and besides Jimmie, Manny's sister, cuddled
him like a doll. We arrived, winded, to find him relaxed
behind the steering wheel, his putt-putting lips going full
blast down some mountain road only he could navigate.

A sense of loss was lifted from me, however momentarily.
A sense of gain and joy took its place. The whole episode
is a vivid recollection that keeps returning periodically for
no reason that I know of except that Sonny's loss, although
temporary, brought home to me at age nine a certain horror
that would stay with me for a lifetime, the horror of utter
dissolution. The fear I had felt sweep over me there where
the spring flowed into the creek was one that took heart,
head, limbs and scattered them into a neverending night of
loss. I don't think I have ever had that feeling since, of the
heart sinking out and away from my body.

For Roland, Presumed Taken

By the time we missed you dusk was settling in.
The first reaction was to think
of drowning, the deep hole just north of the house
that the spring flows into
out from under the sycamore.
You had played there earlier in the day
and had wanted to wade the still water
after minnows schooling the shadows.

We tracked you back to the spring, and I died
with fear that you would be floating
among the lilies, white as the ghost of fish.

But your tracks veered left
toward the valley where the cattle grazed,
then vanished in the flowing grass.
I blew the horn that called the cattle in.
You knew the sound and loved the way
the cattle came loping up at feeding time.

Roland, still, today, you cannot hear the sound of the horn,
cannot holler back up the mountainside
to let us know in your wee voice you are safe and found.
Why you walked off into the green of that day
we can never know, except the valley
and the mountain beyond must have yielded a sudden
sound or flash of light that took your eyes away.
And you were gone. It is as if

eagles swooped you up, leaving
not one trace to tell us the way you went away.
Nights I imagine the beat of drums,
the clanging of toy swords,
rocking horses neighing
on their tracks.
In another age
I would offer
up my glove
to God
to have you back.

Now, we have packed away your life
in boxes we store
in case the memory

we hold is swept away
by chance
or the slow years.

The sound of dogs howling at night does strange things to my psyche: memory floods with a rush of wind, and I am back to the house in Holson Valley. I am in bed, looking out a low window: there is a full moon with a bright star near its bottom tip. Colonel and Butch are wailing mournfully, and then they are engaged in some fight to the death with an unknown intruder.

For days word spread along the valley that a rabid dog was on the loose. My father had not penned our two dogs because, during the day, they were always with him, and he liked the protection they provided against snakes. At night they were left loose much for the same reason, to sleep on the open porch of the house. I think he blamed himself for the loss of those dogs until the day he died.

It took fourteen days from the time we penned Colonel for him to go mad, and fifteen for Butch. The stately collie turned surly and slobbering and threatened whoever or whatever approached him with eyes devoid of any remembrance of things past. We didn't want to believe he had rabies and waited a day to make sure. By the next morning Butch, too, was mad. The half-feist half-mongrel was completely debilitated, fouling himself with a stench no one could stand. I was not allowed to watch, but I can still hear the sound of the .410 shotgun my father used on both dogs. There were the two blasts, followed by the bells of the Holson Valley Church: it was Sunday. Every dog I ever had for the remainder of my childhood and adolescence I called Butch out of reverence for what had happened to the two dogs, which had always been a part of the family, at least from my small vantage point in time.

The fear of rabies was very real in eastern Oklahoma when I was growing up. Though vaccine was available, it was a far piece to get access to it: Fort Smith was fifty miles to the north and the hospitals at Talihina were poorly supplied. No one vaccinated animals against rabies that I knew of. Yet everyone knew stories about someone going mad from the bite of a rabid dog, mad skunk, or raging racoon. Somewhere out of the range of my existence, a valley resident had been bitten by a dog known to have been rabid. He had lain twenty-one days in the Indian hospital in Talihina and had been given as many hypodermic injections, each in his stomach—a horror story that any child would remember and thus would be wary of strange dogs.

Dog Days

I dread the sultry August when days get short
and shadows long creep out to the mountains of the east,
when the dance of heat is seen far down the road,
when rivers no longer run but squat like turtles in their
    scummy houses.

For it is then that the dog trails my shadow,
his swollen tongue dragging dust,
a growl hidden behind filmy eyes;
when I stop, he stops, half within my shadow;
when I move, he moves, in step.

I dread the sultry August when days get short
and the sun seems a ball of fire-froth,
slithering from the jaws of the rabid beast
of sulky summer days
and my shadow lengthens and the dog is there.

In those days, as far back in the hills as we were, I doubt
anyone really knew the difference between rabies and distemper. Both were deadly and debilitating. The big difference is, of course, that distemper is not harmful to humans
in any real sense of the word. The valley people could have
comforted their many animals afflicted with distemper and
saved even more, rather than shunning them until they died
or blasting their brains out, if they had known the difference
between the symptoms of the two diseases. My father, years
after killing the two dogs, became convinced that they had
only distemper and could have been saved. They could not
of course have been, even if it had been distemper, for by
the time the symptoms show up the animal is lost. No, the
dogs were mad: I can still see the eyes and the snarling,
frothing mouths. It had been said that we learn everything
too late to save us from grief. It is still being said.

Dogs were important for us during the Holson Valley and
the Summerfield years. Small game was plentiful, but you
needed a good squirrel or rabbit dog to save time. To still-
hunt, as I often did in my early teens, took hours of patient
waiting to bag a squirrel, and rabbits would freeze in their
tracks in the brush, making detection next to impossible.
Olivie Wann, a native of Summerfield and survivor of Iwo
Jima, was the best still-hunter that I have ever known: he
would sit for hours with his back rigid against the bark of
a red oak in wait for squirrels to become convinced he was
a natural object. There was not a day that he chose to hunt
squirrels that he did not bag as many as he wished, usually
one or two young ones (he would say) for the frying pan,

for he knew the lay of the land and the way of the wild. He liked to hunt the deep woods of the river bottoms just northwest of the old Fourche Maline bridge and immediately east of what is in the local vernacular called the Slab, a strip of paved road, long ago abandoned, about a quarter mile long. The woods were filled with tall oaks and hickories and free of much underbrush because of the thick canopy of limbs and leaves.

The woods on the slopes of Winding Stair and Blue mountains, however, were thick with underbrush except in those rare places where virgin timber stood. We had to have squirrel and rabbit dogs to survive, a fact of life, the simple economics of existence. I was going hunting with my father before I had the strength to carry the single-shot Richardson-Harrington .410 that my grandfather Lewis Barnes had left me. It was a wonderful routine: I would walk always behind my father, and he would follow the dog or dogs, which always fanned out some fifty to a hundred yards ahead of us, and usually uphill. When the dog picked up a trail, he would usually break into a fast trot or, if the trail were really fresh, into a dead run, and we would follow as fast as we could. There was always a danger of losing the squirrel if he leaped from treetop to treetop. The dog would remain treed at the base of the trunk of whichever tree the squirrel went up, and we might or might not be able to find him in the density of blackjacks and pines above us. If the dog treed the squirrel clean, which is to say up one tree, then it was my job to go to the side of the tree opposite my father and shake a low bush. The action would scare the squirrel around the tree and thus give my father a clear shot at him.

Like Olivie Wann, we never hunted for the thrill of it. We took only what we needed from the wild, and I suspect we were more reverent about it than I remember being. I do not remember apologizing to the squirrel for killing it, but

I do remember feeling shame for killing in order to eat. At
an early point in my life, I thought the feeling a weakness.
Now I know it was a strength.

Hunting Winding Stair Mountain

The sky overcast, a threat of thunder
murmuring up the heavy south kept us
from hearing the trailing hound until the rush
of wind our way told that he had treed more

than we had set out to find on that day.
The forest of oaks and knotty pines obscured
even more the hazed sun we thought we had
a bearing on. I knew the dog would die

if the three coons decided he was no
real threat. With one shot my father took
the smallest one. Climbing, the others shook
with rage across the canopy of low

pines. I know we did not hunt for the sport
of it. I long ago forgave my father
for whatever sin it was that I swore
we were being punished for when we heard

the lightning strike the tree the dog still barked
up. The silence that followed filling the woods
I can't remember feeling since. We could
not find our way under the impending dark

that kept us from keeping the mountain at
our backs. The rain pelted us with some fierce
determination. We did not know north
from south, east from west, up from down, nor that

night was yet hours away. When the sky did
lift, the mountain loomed upon us like the storm.
We had not known it lay so close to home
that we could be halfway up the darker side

waiting for the moon or sun to take us down.
The old dog smelled of burning sulfur all
the way down the steep slopes on our slow heels,
his eyes surprised still by the god of coons.

  Later, I would ask the forgiveness of all the animals I have
killed for food or warmth. It is the thing to do. I will continue
to eat their meat and wear their skins, but now in reverence
and full knowledge of what I am doing.

By the time I started high school, we had moved back to within three hundred yards of the place where I was born, a short mile and a half from Summerfield. By this time, the house of my birth had been destroyed by fire and the weeds had even obliterated traces of the foundation, which had been simply a few flat rocks upon which the joists had rested.

For the first two years of high school I walked to and from Summerfield to catch the schoolbus to LeFlore, seven miles to the west. Every morning and afternoon I would take a shortcut, to shave a quarter mile off the walk, through Jack Curtis's fields and meadow, past the mound where my brother had heard the moan. The mound, guarded by oaks and sassafras, for a long while gave me an eerie feeling when I passed by, but gradually I became accustomed to it and could even walk by it at night without too much of a tingling at the back of my neck.

A quarter mile to the northwest of the mound, however, was an old place that I steered clear of. My mother had told me that her elder sister who died in 1944, Aunt Mae, had lived there during the World War I years. It was a steep round hill, wooded up to the top, which was a circular clearing with a diameter of about a hundred yards. The

house had long since rotted down, and only the outline of a few rotting logs remained, along with some twisted, rusted corrugated tin sheets covering the opening of a deep hand-dug well lined with stones. Someone, she told me, had fallen into the well and drowned. She was vague on this point, but it made a lasting impression upon my psyche. I always gave the top of the hill a wide berth and coasted around its base whenever I had to go to the west pasture after our milch cow in the early evenings.

One evening in late summer the milch cow had been particularly bent on staying in the pasture, and no matter how insistent I was that she take the trail home she kept trying to cut back to the good grazing along the branch. I managed, after chunking several clods of dirt at her, to get her headed in the right direction until we came to the base of the hill. She bolted straight up it. I had little choice except to follow her.

By the time I reached the top, she was nowhere in sight and I was winded. I sat down on a rock to rest for a few minutes, listening for her sounds in the woods at the edge of the clearing, and heard nothing for what seemed a long while. Then came the sound of a harmonica, as if coming from the middle of the clearing—faint but unmistakenly, the clear notes of a slow, sad tune. I looked around from where I sat, thinking I would see someone. I saw nothing, heard nothing except the notes of a harmonica. The sound was centered in the clearing. There was nothing in the clearing except the well and the tall grass waving in the slight breeze from the south. I felt the hairs on my arms and the back of my neck rise. None of our three or four neighbors could play a harmonica. I was the only one who could.

That dusk had begun to fall and a light wind had risen in the trees did not help matters. I was frightened as a child is frightened by dark tales. I felt a presence about me that

I could not name. Then just as quickly as the fear had come it rolled away in a soft wave, and I sat there listening to the song of the harmonica on the wind. I must have remained there for the better part of an hour, for when I walked back down the hill and on to our barnyard, stars had begun to come out and my mother was milking the cow, which obviously had decided the barn lot was where she ought to be. I could hear the *pling-pling* of the first squirts of milk in the bottom of the bucket as I climbed over the fence at the back of the barn.

I could never adequately explain hearing that sound of a harmonica to myself, though I do know that certain sounds would carry for miles in the closing light of day, echoing off hill and hollow. At dusk, when the wind begins to fall and all the birds find their roosts, there is something holy about the day. It is a quiet time in the country around Summerfield when you can almost hear the living earth itself, and words spoken or sung in the moments before full dark seem to go floating on and on forever just above the ground toward some destination only the words may know.

It is a time in the summer, after supper, when you are doing last chores outside, a time when you hear the opening hoots of owls down the hollows and the rubbing chirps of crickets in the barn, a time when the bark of a dog is answered by another a mile away. It is a time when you might feel the wake of the wings of a late hawk and hear the rustle of field mice in hedgerows. It is a time that moves inexorably toward sleep under the stillness of moon or cloud.

There is a photograph that has haunted me for fifty years. In the foreground the prone body of a dead man. Kneeling beside the body, a man with some sort of cloth in one hand, as if he had just taken it away from the dead man's face, and in the other hand a slim and deadly Spencer rifle. Or perhaps the rifle is lying on the same blanket as the dead man. Perhaps I remember wrong. The particulars of the photograph seem to be shifting with memory, as if the picture is somehow in motion, a slow movement in time.

The picture first appeared at the bottom of the wall-length mirror in Harley's Barbershop, in Wister, where I got my first professional haircut (some while after a neighbor, Cliff Singleterry, peeled my head when I told him I wanted a GI). Every time I had my hair cut I would sit looking at the picture while Harley hacked away and talked with his cronies who were always there smoking or chewing and waiting for their next welfare check to arrive. When finally I asked about the picture, which obviously was a tintype, Harley said that it was the photograph of the last legal execution by firing squad in Indian Territory and it had taken place in Red Oak, some twenty miles to the west of Wister. I am certain that it was an original photograph.

The kneeling sheriff or deputy looks toward the camera. His hand holding the cloth is suspended in midair. He has done what he has had to do. Neither pain nor regret nor pleasure is in his eyes. All expression seems to have faded out of his face. The downed man is serene, content with lying there on the blanket, which seems spread for a midday nap. There are six, maybe seven, men standing in a semicircle, all looking at the camera but with full knowledge—and this you can read on their faces—of the dead man's guilt.

Why, periodically, I recall that photograph I will never know. There was no horror about it. All was quiet acceptance of the way things were: the body, the kneeling man, the onlookers, the long rifle. But across the years the image would flash forth at odd times and I would once again be sitting there in the barber's chair, facing the mirror, and the picture stuck fast at the mirror's bottom right-hand corner.

In the spring of 1980, when Carolyn and our younger son, Blake, and I were driving through northern Arkansas on the way to visit my mother and father in Oklahoma, we stopped in Berryville, Arkansas, for lunch. We decided, since we were there, to visit the Berryville Gun Museum. It must have the largest collection of frontier pistols in America. By the exit was a large glass case containing more pistols and old newspaper clippings. There drawing my eyes down to it was a reproduction, in newsprint, of the photograph of the last legal execution by firing squad in Indian Territory. The caption gave the date and location: 1894, Red Oak, Oklahoma.

The haunting would not end with that appearance. A few years later I was on the campus of the University of Oklahoma and, on a whim, decided to walk through the photographic archives. The first photograph my eyes fell on was the same, but this time vastly enlarged.

Two years ago Rilla Askew's fine work of fiction *Strange Business* was published by Viking Penguin. And there in some of the best fiction ever written by an Oklahoman is the scene. Once again: the executed man, the sheriff, the onlookers, the deadly rifle. And there amongst it all: the name, the reason, the explanation of it all.

September 15, 1994: I am reading Angie Debo's *The Rise and Fall of the Choctaw Republic* and the story continues. Silan Lewis was one of a group of men who took part in several political assassinations in the years of 1892 and 1893, when the Choctaw Nation was struggling for national autonomy. Of the accused conspirators, nine were sentenced to be shot. Only one of their number was ever executed: Silan Lewis, on November 5, 1894. The judge in the trial was H. J. Holson of the Choctaw criminal court, the same Judge Holson whose name was given to the creek and the valley some twenty miles southeast of Red Oak.

Debo writes that Silan Lewis "was a fullblood about fifty-four years old who had once been sheriff of his county. He met death like an old-time Choctaw, refusing to take advantage of the comparative freedom that was allowed him, and walking in from the woods in time for his execution. A threatened uprising in his behalf did not materialize, probably because he did not encourage it. His eight companions were dismissed and allowed to leave for the Chickasaw Nation."

An Ex-Deputy Sheriff Remembers the Eastern Oklahoma Murderers

i. Summerfield
They took a tire tool to his head,
this gentle stranger from Wyoming.
Oh, we caught them over
at Talihina drinking beer
at Lester's Place, calling
the myna bird bad names
and shooting shuffleboard.

I'm telling you
they were meek in the muzzle
of our guns. They claimed innocence
and: why, they went fishing
with the cowboy just the other day.
We said we knew, knew too
the way they stole him blind
that night. We spoke of blood,
the way the dogs had lapped his face.
The youngest of the three bad brothers,
barely thirteen, began to cry:
"He told us everything was all right
and we hit him till he died."
And that is how it was,
a simple thing, like breathing,
they hit him until he died,
until he bled Wyoming dry
there on the road
in that part of Oklahoma
no stranger has ever owned.

ii. Red Oak
We shot the Choctaw way back in '94,
last legal execution by firing squad.
He didn't die, through the heart, square
and he didn't die.
The high sheriff, my old boss,
stuffed his own shirt down
the Choctaw's neck
to stop the rattle in his throat.
You couldn't shoot a downed man
no matter what and he had to die.
Damned good Choctaw, I'll say that.

Red Oak had no jail and it was too
blasted cruel to execute him
before his crop was in. The judge
scheduled it for the fall, first Saturday
after the corn was in the Choctaw's crib.
That damned fool Choctaw gathered
his corn like any other dirt farmer,
dressed clean, and kept his word.
"I'm ready" is all he said that day.
You got to admire a man like that,
Indian or not, murderer or just plain fool.
He'd shot three men for sleeping
in his barn and taking the milk bucket
away from his little girl, though she
wasn't harmed at all, and he showed up
just like he'd said he would.
                                    There
was a picnic in the shade after we choked
the Choctaw to death and took the rifle home.
First time I'd ever seen a camera,
big damned black thing on legs,
smelled like seven kinds of sin every time
it popped. Had fresh hominy and chicken and the last
of some damned fine late sweet red watermelons.

iii. LeFlore
Goddamnest thing I ever saw
was when old Mac ran down that poor old LeFlore boy.
Old Mac was drunk as thunder
when we chained him to the tree
he'd just pissed on back of his house.
Said he'd wanted to see what it was like
to bounce a man off the hood
of the truck he hauled pulpwood on.

No other reason than just that.
Hell of a note, but I've heard worse.
They all have got some sort of song and dance.
Old Mac's kids were screaming louder
than the crows and threatening us with garden hoes.
We shooed them off with fake fast draws.
That poor old LeFlore boy was as deaf as stone,
a condition they say came with the color of his skin,
though as mild in his ways as the first fall winds.
Old Mac had hit him from behind. Coming
down the gravel road, lord, he must have been
doing sixty and with a full two-cord load.
Hit him dead on. Center. Cracked his
back in half all the way through. That poor
old LeFlore boy's rubber boots were left
standing exactly where he last had stood.
How can you account for that, those silly
rubber boots standing bolt upright
dead in the middle of the goddamned road?

iv. Wister
What made him think he could get away with it
is beyond me. Hell, he'd lived over at Glendale
all his life. Everybody knew he had a stiff
little finger on his right hand. The mask hid
nothing, not even the fear and tobacco juice
he always drooled out the corners of his mouth.
He shot the teller right between the eyes and
made the others strip. Don't ask why. Cleaned
our the vault of a thousand dollars, mostly
fives, and made it fifty yards down the Frisco
tracks before Mathes, the bank's owner, naked
as a jaybird and pissing a blue streak, blew

his left shoulder off with a 30.06. I've got
the cartridge shell to this day. Was going to
have one of them little lighters, size of your
finger, made out of it. But I decided to quit.

Fox hunting, Oklahoma style, was the favorite pastime of the old men, and a few of the younger ones, of Summerfield all the years that we lived there. The few times I was allowed to go with the "old ones," I could see that the event was highly ritualistic, not that anyone was conscious of any rules whatsoever. It is just that the hunt always began, proceeded, and ended in the same way. With fox hunting English style, traditionally you have daylight, horses, hounds, and horns. Oklahoma style, you have night, a campfire, old stories, and the music of the trailing hounds.

Sundown on certain appointed days of spring, summer, or fall, sitting on the wooden bench on the concrete slab of Dooley Evans's DX station, you could see down the road to the south a few hundred feet Bob Smith loading into his pickup a gaggle of hounds—blueticks, redbones, black and tans, and even a beagle or two. Before he finished loading, at least four or five other pickups would join his at the side of the road. At times there were as many as twenty or twenty-five dogs involved in the hunt.

The regulars were, besides Bob, Leo (Bob's son), Paul Deere, Bill Hollan, and Sam Johnson. Others joined from time to time, as the old ones died, but the core group always seemed the same. That is, it always had the same attitudes, the same stories, the same fierce determination to do what it had always done.

The hunters knew the terrain, knew the valleys and the canyons, the high ground and the low, where the rivers ran, and the confluences of all the branches. From any spot on any given night of a hunt any one of the group could identify a trailing hound by yelp and bay within a radius of five miles and could tell you the exact location of the trailing hound and the direction of the chase and its twists and turns—an amazing knowledge of land and animal behavior that I could never master.

The hunt usually took place in the hills to the south of Summerfield, and nearly always the campfire would be on high ground a mile or so either direction, east or west, off the Holson Valley Road or sometimes off Highway 271, which connected Talihina with Poteau and ran through the middle of Summerfield in the old days before the state highway department moved it a mile to the west to bypass the town. Hunters and dogs would sit around the campfire until full dark. Then one or more of the hunters would take all the dogs to a designated point miles away, and the general theory was that the dogs, then, would pick up a fox's scent and chase it west to east, north to south, whatever direction past the fire and off into the far reaches of the night. There was never any intention that the dogs should catch, or tree, the fox. The enjoyment was in the chase, for the dogs and the hunters. The dogs doing the work, the hunters would sit around the fire with the kind of intensity about their ears that would be hard indeed to explain to an outsider. The sound of the trailing hounds, down through the hollows and up through the hills, baying, barking, their voices ringing with the excitement of the chase, never quite attaining, yet always gaining on their prey—this was a rhapsody no one could record. They listened to the hounds in a kind of knowing ecstacy that I have never seen since. It was a kind of reverence that every artist prays for in relation to his work.

By midnight the chase would be over: the dogs would be called in, at least those near enough to hear the low-frequency sound of a bull's hollowed-out horn, which every head of household had. That was one of the first things I wanted to make as soon as I was old enough to hunt any game, a horn like my father's to call the dogs in when I had my limit of squirrels or rabbits and the hunt was over. (The sounds of low-frequency horns carry much farther than, say, the sounds of high-pitched whistles.) The fox hounds that were out of range, which many very often were, would be called again in the morning after the hunters had had a good night's sleep at home and breakfast. Most of the hounds that spent the night out would return to site of the campfire, or in some instances would come all the way home after a weary night in the hills.

On the Mountain

The hide is nailed
upon the door.

The old bitch strains,
licks a sore forepaw.

The pup trails asleep,
hounds a first
wild hunt into
his hell of dream.

A low wind
lifts the dust
up off the floor,
inches it
toward the fire.

The pup runs
a spastic course,
freezes and bays
himself half awake.

The wind dies down;
the fire sparks out.

The old bitch groans
herself to sleep.

The hide is nailed
upon the door.

On those nights when the dogs failed to pick up the scent of a fox and silence reigned, or when they erroneously went after a timber wolf and rapidly, silently ran with him straight into the next county or the next state, stories were the thing, stories that would make your hair stand on end or set your teeth on edge with the copper taste of fear, stories that chronicled human, subhuman, superhuman endeavor from the San Bois to the Kiamichi, from Rich Mountain to Muddy Boggy. On those few times I was privileged to go on the hunt, I sat in the circle and learned, and I am hearing still those stories and hearing still the trailing, baying hounds whose chase I never want to end, nor will it end as long as memory runs.

Wolf Hunting near Nashoba
—for Paul Deere and Leo Smith

Nights you wake to sudden stars
and wind that's always on the run.
Hard hills hugging sulfur springs
make echoes leap past your tuning ears.

You turn your collar up and square
your butt into the stone-dead earth
to better feel the oblique sounds at first,
a thirst of bones no mountain waters clear.

The hounds are scaling up the mouths.
The beagle beat is a bit irregular,
but sweet as madrigals in a greening air.
A comet splits the sky from north to south.

You hear yourself yell the bluetick straight
to hell with *go*. Two other dead stars fall.
You count the losing hounds over a hogbacked hill,
eject a cartridge you've lately come to hate.

Times like this you'd like to end it
all. Kill wolf and dogs and shoot the stars.
The thought passes with the chase. At your
feet the fire you forgot you ever lit is out.

Fox hunting in our neck of the woods is a thing of the
past. The master of the hounds, Bob Smith, is dead. Leo is
dead. Nearly all the others who, during those slow years I
was rooted in place, formed the circle of hunters have died
or faded into the obscurity of extreme old age. Death and
slow memory take their toll. The old ones are truly old now.

In my mind, when I knew them, they were in their prime, middle-aged or young men full of the necessity of time— that is, hot to do the things they knew they were meant to do. Wrongheaded as they may have often been and without formal education, they nonetheless passed on what they knew by doing the things they had to do. They go with me, those old fox hunters, wherever I go. And I am richer because of it.

Little is known of my maternal grandparents, Joseph Adams and Lalie Ruth Fredonia Nutt. For Grandfather Joseph and Grandmother Lalie, then, these few words. Joseph, his sister, and their mother and father crossed over from Wales and landed at Savannah, Georgia, sometime in 1867, presumably in spring or summer, when Joseph was about ten years old, for they then set out on foot for western Mississippi, settling somewhere around Yazoo City or Natchez. Eventually, Joseph married Lalie, who was one half Choctaw, and they had seven children: Ethel, Lou, Mae, Oliver, Weaver, Charles (called Jack), and Bessie.

Lalie was the daughter of Dr. Nutt, a Civil War physician, a Confederate officer who lost his fortune because of the war. Whether he was the fullblood Choctaw or his wife, whose name is forgotten, no one now can say. We know almost nothing about Lalie's parents. There is some evidence, though it is indeed sketchy, that it was our Dr. Nutt who started Longwood Mansion and left it unfinished because of the outbreak of the war. (Today the mansion is a state park, with the workmen's tools lying where they had been dropped at news of the conflict.) Before her death in 1985, my mother told me that there was a settlement from the Nutt estate that came to the descendants of Dr. Nutt in the 1910s. As she recalled, it was not very much at all, just a few dollars for each of the surviving grandchildren of Dr. Nutt.

Most of the children of Joseph and Lalie must have been born in Mississippi and East Texas (around Tyler). My mother, however, was born near Summerfield, in Indian Territory, in a house next to the trees in the middle of the field, where lies the mound the good-for-nothings dug into those many years ago.

There were several migratory moves on Joseph and Lalie's part. The first they made together was to East Texas. From there they moved to Colorado in the late 1880s, where they raised vegetables and sold them to miners on the eastern slopes of the Rockies. But Joseph, by all the few accounts we have, was, whenever he could find a position, a Baptist minister. Preachers with large families, however, had to supplement their income as best they could. Many were farmers as well as preachers.

By at least 1899 Joseph and Lalie were in Oklahoma, near Summerfield, for my mother's birth. Little remains of the stories that would have made the years of migration mean-ingful. My uncle Weaver knew a few, but they were vague of outline to begin with and now have faded too far into the recesses of memory to recall. One thing I distinctly recall my mother noting, which was corroborated by both my uncles, Weaver and Oliver, is that Joseph and Lalie made the trip to Colorado from Texas by ox cart. Both died in an influenza epidemic that ravaged eastern Indian Territory in the winter of 1903 and are buried in the Summerfield Cemetery.

The Family Plot

They tried to get me, one and all,
to go to church, sit on the front-row

pew, pray. I feigned indifference to
God and man. Oh, secretly though
I was awed by the graveyard through
which I ran when moon and owl

both were dark and I late for home.
Only the lateness of the hour
made me a boy brave enough then
to take the shortcut through flowers,
stone slabs of unacknowledged sin,
the REQUIESCAT IN PACE blown

in the unrelenting wind. I knew
the stones that lined the path by heart,
not by head, and was struck, changed
by windy death each time the start
of night bird or stalking beast ranged
up the length of spine and through

my hair. Dead uncles, aunts, deacons,
all spelled death and I would have none
of that. Father, mother, brother,
sister, cousins, all woebegone
because they knew how much I'd rather
sing hillbilly than their true songs.

I hid my crazy fear of death
to all except the limbo souls
along the path I'd sometimes take:
only the shades could know my palms
were cold from more than cold, the ache
of aging in my living breath.

    Bill Nutt, Lalie's brother, came to Oklahoma to join Lalie
and Joseph, and eventually got into serious trouble in Ada

and was sentenced to life imprisonment for murder. He was known to prison authorities as Wild Bill Nutt. In time he was made a trustee, and was even in many instances sent on armed manhunts for escapees from the prison at McAlester. On these occasions he did from time to time visit my mother and her siblings fifty miles to the east, in Summerfield. There was a story about him my mother used to be fond of telling, though she was very serious in telling it. She made it clear that it was exactly the way he told it to her.

Bill Nutt was a bad man in his youth. He committed foul sins. It was not until he was in prison that he saw the light of goodness, and that happened one night when, as a trustee, he strapped on the prison-issue pistols and rode off into the cross-timbered country southwest of McAlester, looking for two escaped convicts. He had brought back six men in the past, three of whom had been shot squarely between the eyes. On this particular night, somewhere north of Antlers, he was riding a strong long-legged dun down a narrow fenced lane leading to he knew not where, except somewhere far up ahead there was a pinpoint of light that must have been a ranch house. Tree limbs brushed his face. And then out of the darkness surrounding him, something fell solidly onto the back of the horse and gripped Wild Bill's shoulders. The horse reared and screamed an unearthly cry and plunged into the deep night. Wild Bill froze, petrified in the saddle. A man who was afraid of nothing turned almost to stone. The horse bolted toward the light, and in the faint glow of the farm lantern hanging on a gate post Wild Bill Nutt saw the white boney skeletal hand on his shoulder. And then it left in a rush of wind. The horse pulled up short, wild and winded, its nose frosting the lantern's globe. From that night on Wild Bill Nutt was a changed man. He killed no more, though he continued to track men down for the prison authorities. This was my mother's story,

and I believed her. Wild Bill Nutt died in McAlester Prison,
serving hard time.

Autobiography, Chapter V: Ghost Town

Boards the shape of shadows, windows blued by the
    awful
        sun, the black hollow of gone doors, and always the
        constant sound of wind.

You try to take this absent town in one bound of soul,
        afraid you'll stumble on the derelict years only
        the headstones name.

You fail. The mind finds a stop: a rainbow in broken
        glass, a stream of dust in the washed-out street,
        footsteps you can't possibly hear.

The half saloon bangs its half a door the wind walks
        through. Night falls like hail, down with the
        thirsting hills.

You spread your blankets before the blank eyes of the
        town and lie in wait, a poor thief, for the permanence
        of stars. Inside your throat hangs a silence: there
        are no words, no words.

Home for me will always remain the Great Southwest, even though at this point in time I have spent the last twenty-four years in northern Missouri. That the Southwest is a rich cultural region, few will deny. But what its boundaries are is a moot question. For William Bartram in his *Travels* in the early 1700s, the old Southwest was Alabama, Mississippi, Louisiana. But this did not last. In later years Washington Irving showed us Arkansas and eastern Oklahoma as Southwest territory. Cherokee-souled Sam Houston took us to Texas. The Santa Fe Trail opened up New Mexico, and the region expanded on to California. Useless to argue boundaries.

But there are things in my lifetime I cannot help associating with the term *Southwest*. My grade school geography and history classes taught me that Oklahoma, Texas, and New Mexico were the Southwest. My high school library had one book that was passed off as Southwest literature— J. Frank Dobie's *Coronado's Children*, a book that made me dream of buried treasure from the Brazos River to the Superstition Mountains. He made it all come alive, that feeling for West Texas and Oklahoma, and he did it through his characters, the spinners of tall tales, Coronado's children.

The cultural Southwest means always for me Indians, their land and their customs and their languages. The Native American languages are going fast. It is no small wonder that they have held out this long. There are mighty few Yuchi speakers left today. Ten or twelve years ago, I believe, there were some two hundred acknowledged Oklahoma Yuchis living, and of those perhaps four or five native speakers. How many languages we have lost! The Yuchis, who came from Georgia with the Creeks in forced migration, are virtually no more. That great tribe believed that they came from the East, across a great water—a belief that seems borne out by the so-called Metcalf stone that was unearthed in Georgia back in the 1960s bearing characters from the Phoenician alphabet.

Some years ago I spent several hours with one of the few remaining Yuchi speakers, little girl who was learning the language from her aged grandmother. I listened to her and tried to transcribe a few phrases of the language. I remember her saying that the typical greeting in Yuchi is "Wa-hin-gi?" (Where are you going?) or "Sen-ga-le-la?" (How are you?) She spoke of many things Yuchi: I tried to transcribe. Several days later we met, and she greeted me with "Sen-ga-le-la?" Wanting to appear miraculously fluent, I replied, with the only phrase I could remember then, "Yubo-ah-tee-tee-onde-de-tah," which means "I want an orange." She laughed long and hard, then said, "You must try harder." Words I try to hang on to.

Under Buffalo Mountain

The prairie flows toward
the sacred lake

where the silent water
waits, deep

in its secret of geese,
for the coming of snow.

Here the Choctaw stopped, forever,
staked the ground

with bones broken beyond rage.
Blood hides

in these hills and haunts
the faded town:

the drunk drowns in sleep,
the geese forget to come,

the snow falls,
and the moon is down.

Tomorrow we will be able to count the fluent Choctaws on one hand if something is not done today. I was raised in Choctaw country, LeFlore County, and count myself one-eighth *Chahta*. I was raised on the language and the foods, practically all that was left us then of the culture. I have eaten *chongkus chom pooey* (pork backbone boiled in hominy) and *tom fuller* (meat and cornmeal cooked in a cornshuck) and hickory nut soup—to my infinite delight. But now these have passed away like so many other things Choctaw. In a few years Choctaw will become a rare language. I hate to see that happen, but it is bound to come to that unless something more is done soon. I can recall the day when "Halito, chin achukma?" (Hello, how's your fat?) was a familiar greeting in eastern Oklahoma, around Talihina and Summerfield. You will find few replies to the question today.

I am proud of the Choctaw blood I carry, and I am equally
proud of the Welsh blood in my veins. But I object to the
term *regional writer* or *ethnic writer* or even *Native American
writer*, though it may apply to a number of us in a general
sense. I don't think I could be called a Kiamichi poet or an
Oklahoma writer by any far stretch of the imagination. In
my work, place-names are important, but they are usually
important not because of any geographical sense alone but
more so because of the names themselves. "Antlers," for
example, in "Stopping on Kiamichi Mountain" (*The American
Book of the Dead*), carries with it the name of a very old town
in Oklahoma but also a pretty good-sized rack of horns. So
if I use "Antlers," it is because I can get mileage out of the
image as well as the place-name. A poet not too long ago
came out with a very short poem—and I thought a very
bad poem in a very good magazine—and one or two lines
went something like this: "Spoon, spoon, I love the sound
of spoon." I guess that is the way I feel about many of
the place-names in Oklahoma and elsewhere: the *sounds*
are good.

In Memory of a Day Nobody Remembers: 26 September 1874

Who is left to recall the sacred earth
where Poor Buffalo bit the dust?

The dance of days is the only dance.
Town Indians drunk on Chock and Thunderbird

can never know they were born of a hollow log
or the ritual of the sacred sun dance doll.

Nobody can recall the massacre
of men, and horses dead in Tule Creek.

The racial memory fades. O son of man,
what anvil hand forged your soul and skin?

Isatai, who promised to vomit bullets
at Adobe Walls, would have you dance again.

Or Maman-ti, who willed the death
of white-tongued Tay-nay-angopte.

Exploded bones fuse with sand. No grass grows.
Of the chinaberry trees, just one or two.

Palo Duro Canyon: echoes also fade.
K'ya-been's bones lie buried in the bluff.

Dance, ghosts, among the yellow leaves
before they turn to dust.

As a literary magazine editor, professor, writer-in-residence, and lover of good literature, I don't care who writes
the poem, where it is written, or what it is even written
about. Whenever the universal grows out of the specific and
vision is achieved, you can tell yourself here is art and it
should be preserved. Such a work is, for example, N. Scott
Momaday's *House Made of Dawn*. I doubt anyone would call
Momaday a Southwest writer (true, by blood he is largely
Kiowa); his novel deals with the people and the land of New
Mexico, but also Arizona, Oklahoma, southern California. It
is a book of vanishing Americans in all their many faces,
many skins; it is a book that documents the failure of a way
of life, ways of life, the failure of the individual, of society,

of religion, of myth. It is a book that touches the human heart and head and universalizes the human struggle to survive, to prevail, in this hopped-up, turned-on world. The message is as clear in Momaday's work as it is in Ralph Ellison's *Invisible Man* when Jack the Bear finally realizes that to survive we must change, must reject, must affirm, must love, must hate; we must know that ambivalence is the condition of being human and that we are subjects of loss.

Momaday is hardly *just* a Native American writer. I know of no fuller expression of loss in contemporary American literature than that which is expressed in John Big Bluff Tosamah's Sermon and the Peyote Ritual in *House Made of Dawn*. The celebrants know what is to be done—the world as it is must be admitted, affirmed, but also remade, re-created. The four blasts of the eagle bone whistle to the four great corners of the world. In the beginning there was a sound, a single sound at the very center of the universe. In the agony of stasis, sound comes, the first word and—if we are lucky—the poem as world, the world as poem.

Origin

Find a word
you haven't said or signed.

Farm it through
the very terraces of lung,
the steppes of eyes;
and watch a certain power grow,
an origin, a stem.

For there is a chemistry
to words:

how, for instance,
the saliva rises
to the tongue
as the word forms
like a cake
midthroat;

how, too,
the teeth grow
sharp
as the word
falls from the lips
like a green apple.

Molecular
as helix or hell,
words hold together even
stuff the deaf-mute's made of:
a tree of fingers,
a lace of flesh.

There are several contemporary writers that I associate
with the Southwest—that is, Oklahoma, Texas, New Mexico—though I do not see them as *regional*. Then I ask myself:
Is Albert Goldbarth a Southwest writer, a Southwest Jewish
writer? He has lived and written in Texas and Kansas for
years and has done good (weird) work with the character
of Sam Bass. Is Speer Morgan, from Fort Smith, Arkansas,
a Southwest writer hiding out at the University of Missouri?
His fairly recent *Belle Starr: A Novel* would seem to say yes.
But here he comes with a novel called *Brother Enemy*, a
work set in a Caribbean banana republic. Is Speer Morgan
a Caribbean writer? Or is Winston Weathers a Southwest
writer in scholar's disguise at the University of Tulsa? He

is of Osage heritage, but his works go far beyond both Osage country and Tulsa.

There have been many, many anthologies of Southwest literature and Native American literature to tell us just who are the American Indian writers, just who this and who that, along with pedigree. And there will no doubt be more. But we must not be misled. The writer is first a writer, second a Native American, a black, a Chicano.

There may be works about a place, about a people, by a writer native to the area; but none of this gives anyone the right to catalog or label the works *regional*, *Native American*, *black*, or any other term. Is Ralph Ellison, born in Oklahoma City, a regional writer? Is his work to be listed as black literature only, when it is so universal that it is horrifying? Is his *Invisible Man* a product of his Southwest heritage (Hey, boy!), his Southern heritage (I yam what I yam), his New York heritage (Sibyl, you been raped by Santa Claus)? A writer, whoever he may be, if he believes in art as art, will bring everything to bear upon his art, ethnic or otherwise. The works of Ralph Ellison, N. Scott Momaday, J. Frank Dobie—all are larger than the cultural and geographical boundaries we might try to fence them with.

The four years of high school were wasted on me. In spite of them, however, I learned one thing: how to type. I must have learned others, such as how to diagram sentences and thus better see the grammatical functions of elements within, or how to conjugate verb tenses, or how to spell effectively, though it seems to me I have always known fairly well how language works. You cannot have read voraciously since the age of five without gaining some knowledge of how language behaves on the page and in the mouth. As far back as the first grade something wonderful was happening in my life. Reading was broadening my world. I could not seem to get enough of reading. In fact, in reading class when I finished the first reader I was handed—it was called *The First Grade Reader*—I told Mrs. Scott, the first grade teacher, that I had finished *The First Grade Reader* and I wanted now to be in the second grade so that I could read *The Second Grade Reader*. She simply told me to go ask Irene Box, a second-grade student, where the lesson was. I remember having a silly grin of recognition on my face when finally the looks of my former first-grade peers bore down upon me: I had been promoted even before my first school term had time to get well underway.

But I was taught nothing in high school about how to read, or what to read. I simply read and read, until there was nothing in the LeFlore High library, the size of a small closet, I had not read. My English teachers could recommend nothing, for we had no means of attaining anything beyond what was already on hand—the Hardy Boys, Nancy Drew, a few Zane Greys. We had two real novels, *Huckleberry Finn* and *Tom Sawyer*. The rest was junk reading. I should like to think I sensed it, though I probably did not. At an early age I knew that there were definitely two kinds of literature, one of escape and another of enlightenment, and that sometimes the two kinds got all mixed up, as they did in the Twain novels. It was not until I was out of high school, out of LeFlore County, well out of the state for that matter, that I began the discovery of significant interpretative literature on such a grand scale that I never thought possible.

I do not know that anyone really learned anything that directed his life with any precision during those four years. A couple of my graduating class of sixteen went on to college. Most of the boys went to Tulsa or Oklahoma City or Kansas City to find work in factories. Over half of the girls graduating were married immediately. It is the way things were at that time. One of the class was given an appointment to West Point. He did not stay, but joined the Marines instead, rising eventually to the rank of major. Others did not fare so well, I am afraid. I have seen only two or three of the class of '51 in thirty-four years. No doubt some have died. Or retired. Sometimes it means the same thing. It is the way things are in the hill country of eastern Oklahoma.

Out of sheer boredom I joined the National Guard (Company I, 180th Infantry, 45th Division) during my junior year when I was only fifteen years of age. I had to hitchhike to and from Poteau, twenty-one miles to the north of Summerfield, each Monday night for drill. Payday was every three

months, at ten dollars per month. In 1950 the Guard mobi-
lized for the Korean War. I wanted to go, desperately, but my
wise mother was not about to let that happen. My honorable
discharge reads "Error found in contract," a phrase that
should also be printed across the face of my high school
diploma.

A waste, I said, and I mean it. I was taught nothing.
Neither the love of art, nor the way of the world, nor the
worth of numbers, nor the will to achieve. After high school
I suffered through nearly a decade of bone-breaking labor
before I had the will to reach farther than my grasp and look
beyond my range of vision to a wider world of possibilities.

Still, there are images that come rushing back that I cannot
deny are worth the wasted years. You may think that you
can bury the years, but something will always come back
up, debris hanging on it like rocks. And it is just this debris
that interests me and makes that period of my life have a
kind of meaning I can forgive the gone years for.

Skipping

Something never quite returns when you want
the facts the way you'd like the past to be.
It was our last day together: the sun
was bright, the new grass up, the water right,
and no one cared that we had missed the day.

You can't quite remember getting there, or
which of you did this or that: skipping stones
was in our blood, This was our vague good-bye,
a salute to the world of the narrow stream
we frolicked in and the school two miles away.

You never get it right without the weather:
the May sun warmed our cheeks. We swam till noon.
Then the girls spread lunch on the bank under
the sycamore tree. Above us the Tarzan swing
was a thread of the sun, and we drifted

on a wave of small thought and talk, already
forgetting what we had been those walled years.
But still it's not quite right: you remember
more than was. The love didn't really happen.
You were too shy, or the others were wrapped

up in future selves. You know that someone
almost drowned: two others pulled him out by
the hair. He'd dived too deep. There was a knot
on his crown. Or maybe he'd just faked it
for the tears the girls almost didn't shed.

What is this life? We should have asked stones,
grass, stream. We idled down the sun. The songs
we sang should have echoed off whatever
doom or dance we still beat time to. But they
fade, and the faces come up wrong, the facts

a reconstruction of no consequence. Once
you've done it, you never lose the knack of
skipping flat stones. How smooth the rock feels
against thumb and fingers as you release it
into its final spin and brief buoyancy.

In May 1951 I left Summerfield, quietly telling myself that I had stepped in the last pile of cow dung I ever would. I was going to Oregon, a distant and exotic land of towering trees and mountains always green, of rugged coasts where ships heavy with gold had run aground by the hundreds, where, in other words, a man might make his fortune off the land with no more effort than it took to pick a pebble up off the beach. In a way, I have not lost that childish dream: I still think I live in a time of limitless possibilities. There is still the possibility of that green land beyond the next hill which may be the place I am looking for.

I had lived all my seventeen years either in Summerfield or within a day's walk of the town. I had seen friends leave whom I knew I would not see again, and I knew there was a fatalism holding those who stayed behind with a grip no god could loose. I did not want to stay at home so long that I would know defeat of sense and soul. I knew I had to leave, or be counted among those who were even at my age withering into a complacency of spirit that accepts defeat with little more than a yawn.

Autobiography, Chapter I: Leaving Summerfield

Low wind across old weeds warps your sense of hours;
    the day is heavy with cloud and slow hawks.

The last false front you catch sight of cracks
    the color of old harness, rattles like bone
    chimes in a wind you know you will never
    see clear through.

The road straight out is black with tar oozed
    into itself; fenced against the road, the weeds
    wait out the wire.

The sun has danced upon this town and gone; not
    even a mirage is left to lie you lives you
    sometimes thought you'd live.

There's a distant sound of bells you know don't ring.

The last false front is falling with your years;
    your eyes are webbing with the panes.

You curse the town for all you're worth,
    but know you'll have to come home again,
    fast as a rabid fox, when the years have made
    the town quick with old men's dreams.

   My brother and sister Marveda were both calling Oregon
their homes at this time, and I had been waiting anxiously
for graduation so I could finally join them. They had gone
there just after Marveda's husband, Chet Hamner, and Hack
had gotten out of the service. My brother had been the
first to go, joining my mother's brother, Weaver Adams, in

certain logging ventures in the hills above Dexter and Lowell. By the time I arrived, however, both Hack and Chet
had left logging for heavy construction. Hack was the chief
highline operator on the construction of the massive Lowell
Dam, which was three or four years in the making. Chet
was a catskinner on the same project. It was a time when
work was plentiful for skilled machine operators and unskilled labor, and I had no trouble at all finding work with
Morrison-Knudson and later with Utah Construction, working on the same project as Hack and Chet but doing unskilled
labor, which consisted at first of pulling nails out of used
concrete forms and later, after I had been fired for not denail-
ing fast enough, of cutting blue tops (scooping away the
dirt from survey stakes) so the grader operator could finish
the dirt work on road beds. With hindsight I know those
two jobs were absolute drudgery, though at the time I was
too enthralled with the Pacific Northwest to care what I had
to do to live. I was surrounded by the foothills of the Cascades and the mountains of the coast range, and the great
Willamette Valley that stretched from Portland to Cottage
Grove was a new land I was anxious to explore.

What I liked most about being my own man was the
absolute feeling of freedom that the Pacific Northwest gave
me. I felt that I had escaped a confinement that the accident
of birth had put upon me. I never wanted to return to Oklahoma, where most everything, except the pines, turned
brown or gray in winter. Of course, I would return, and
with pleasure. But that initial feeling of exhilaration, of escape, that feeling of having open country before me, is still
there in the memory of those early days of my nine years
in Oregon.

Even today I get a kind of geographical high when traveling through new territory or revisiting a place I haven't been
for years. It was like Oregon all over again when my wife,

Carolyn, and I went to Italy in 1990 and to Paris the year
before. It was like that when we were in Munich through
the winter months of 1995. I am affected by place. I believe
that anyone who does not somehow reflect place in his
art is not only a fool but also a lost soul. The geophysical
environment of this planet is just too dominant a feature for
any interpretive writer to ignore. He does so at a great risk.

After the Great Plains

Nothing remains the same in this long land.
Bird, fox, gully, grass, all are history
as soon as the moon rises or the wind climbs,
tales told by shadows leaning toward a vista
few eyes discern.

What strikes the windshield hardest as you drive
across is haze, distance claiming being
as absolute as the grasshoppers crushed on
the glass. There is no sameness to a land
that paints itself

different each dawn. The wind in your hair
today becomes a mouse's breath four states
beyond tomorrow. The river you ford could not
be any river. Particular, it flows through
the heart of the land.

After the Great Plains you are not the same.
No matter which way you cross something stays
firmly with you, a sense hard to name, like
a pebble in the toe of your boot you can't shake
out in this life.

From early 1954 through late 1959 I lumberjacked for Giustina Brothers Lumber Company, of Eugene. Most of those years were spent on water, sorting and rafting and scaling (determining the worth of) logs. I loved the work as much as I had loved the rivers of my youth. But after five years I had had enough. I wanted more out of my freedom. What lumberjacking had given me I understood and was grateful for: time to continue reading and to reflect on all that I read. By the end of the 1950s I could discern in literature what I knew to be good or bad or mediocre writing. And by that time, too, I had begun to want to write. I had seen compression and the great art of suggestion over statement in Katherine Anne Porter and Ernest Hemingway. I had sensed the value of structure and myth in Thomas Mann. I had learned that the human heart and mind were nearly always at odds from William Faulkner. I thought I was ready to write. I bought a typewriter and typed a fifty-page novella, in imitation of every bullfighting story Hemingway ever did. No one had to tell me it was bad: in the writing of it I realized that something other than a typewriter and a will to work was needed. I would have to read more than I ever dreamed possible just to be able to keep from writing like those I read. It sounds like a neverending paradox. I think perhaps it is. I know it is true for me.

The best advice I have ever received from the time I first began trying to write was from a man who became my one great friend in Oregon and who has remained steadfastly so for these forty years. Jerry Easterling, who recently retired from his position with the *Salem Capital-Journal*, put his hand on my shoulder one Friday night in the Roundup Tavern, in Creswell, just after Bobo Olsen had coldcocked his opponent in black and white in the corner above our heads, and said: "All this crap about being a writer is meaningless as long as you are sitting here doing nothing except holding that brown bottle in your hand." In other words, write, he said. There is no other way.

I wanted to write short stories. The novella was the first try. Others followed. None succeeded. I thought college was the answer. It was not. I learned nothing about the art of writing there. What I learned about writing I continued to learn from reading the thing itself. If I were ever to write a good short story, I would have to have read enough of them to at least know the possibilities of form, the variables of style, the opportunities of language.

From the mid-1950s through the mid-1960s I wrote eighteen short stories, none of which was good enough even for me to want to send to literary magazines with publication in mind. But then in 1967 I wrote the nineteenth, and I knew I had one good short story. I sent "The Reapers" out for ten years, to forty-nine different literary and general interest magazines, before it was accepted, in the summer of 1978, by the editors of *Sou'wester*. The story has since been anthologized a number of times. Ten years, forty-nine submissions—results like those can cause a writers' psyche to do strange flipflops. I knew I had a damned fine short story when I completed "The Reapers," but I also knew that it was one of the hardest tasks I had ever had before me. Thus I swore I would never write another until I published "The Reapers." And in that interval of ten years, I discovered poetry and found myself at home in form and structure, delighting in the possibilities that both offered. What I had learned from fiction I would apply to poetry on a smaller, even more compressed scale than that of short stories.

Goshen Tavern

Burning my way
through the pitch

dark fog and firs,
I find the tavern
announced by
a normal blue.
Inside:
my eyes ache
from the road.
I drink from
a bottle marked
with mountains.
This is Oregon,
I say, and land
is plenty hard
to know. There
is no one to hear,
but I, exile,
say it anyway.

By the time I left Oregon, in 1959, I think I had learned that freedom is a place of the mind. The work required for earning a living wage was becoming as much a physical prison as I had felt Oklahoma was. I wanted to write, but I had to live, and that required labor on my part that I could not continue to give and survive at a typewriter too. While I had grown free in the mind, I had become a captive of need. I was twenty-six years old when I left Oregon, having worked nearly all the last five years for one company. I left Oregon much for the same reason I left Oklahoma: I felt something dying about me, within me. Though the thrill of the place was still high, I felt that if I did not leave Oregon I would fall into a rut of riotous living that would deaden to the point of annihilation the urge to make stories. I had to change completely the life I was leading of lumberjacking and getting drunk every weekend and doing little else except reading to escape knowing I was caught up in a cycle of lumberjacking and drinking. For I was seeing people around me succumb to habit and addiction. A bartender friend my own age blew his brains out with a 12-gauge shotgun. He could not leave the booze alone. A man I worked with for two years left his wife and five children and, as far as I know, was never heard of again. He simply never returned home one Friday night after his regular weekly poker game with his cronies. Everyone I knew in Oregon was hung up on some routine that appeared to me to be a structure of the damned.

I knew, finally, that I would not find in Oregon what I had left Oklahoma for. I knew at that late age I would like to leave something for the inheritors besides a space on the side of a hill, something of myself yet something beyond what I am. I guess it is, in essence, immortality that every writer wants through his works.

Legacy of Bones

Children from another time
will shake their heads in disbelief
and cautiously brush the dust aside

when they have found at last our bones
upon the hill. And fear that passes
will pass for them upon the hill.

And guessing games that children play
will hold the hour of the day:
a monster hidden in a grove

attacked a lady here at night,
or a traveler from another world
stood lonely vigil here and died.

Our songs will grow dry in the wind
that passes through the mindless moon.
And we, the elders gone, will leave

our marks and knots and stones, but not
the words the children then will chant.
Drawing our bones upon their grids

with tools we never had, they may
pronounce us more than dust again.
For living language makes every-

thing happen, or nothing, as it rides
the tongue into desert places,
solitude where heart still resides.

I returned to Oklahoma reluctantly. Financially, it made sense, even though the University of Oregon had admitted me. It was college that really opened up the world for me. To have unlimited access to thousands of volumes of books and magazines was in itself mind expanding. Three professors at Southeastern State College, in Durant, Oklahoma (now renamed Southeastern Oklahoma State University, or in short, SOSU), had a great deal to do with the course of my life from the time I entered the school in the fall of 1960. Ruth Hatchet, professor of English, convinced me that without keeping the crap detector turned up full blast you could not possibly write anything that was worth keeping. She was a cantankerous old maid who had been lied to by an anxious lover in her youth and ever since trusted nobody who wouldn't look her square in the eye and say, "Yes, ma'am" and "No, ma'am." It was through her tutelage that I began to see the shallowness in much of what was written in contemporary American literature.

Lee Ball, also professor of English, showed me passion in literature, pure flights of ecstacy in Whitman, Jonathan Edwards, Mark Twain, showed me how the language soared when the writer was at his best and how it sagged when he was at his worse. His own feeling for literature was as passionate as anything he read aloud in class. You don't forget people who feel literature alive and jumping within them.

The door to the realm of world literature opened wide when I started college. I majored in English, French, and drama (a triple major). Wade Baskin, my French and German professor, broadened my view of literature to such an extent that I wanted to translate. He allowed a few of us in his classes to assist in the translation of André Gide's *Notebooks of André Walter* and Kurt Kolle's *Introduction to Psychiatry*, which he was doing for the Philosophical Library. It was Wade Baskin who convinced me that I should go to graduate school in comparative literature rather than in drama, or acting. (I seriously thought about becoming a professional actor, for I did well in college dramatics, playing some very good roles very well: Biff in *Death of a Salesman*, the sewerman in *The Madwoman of Chaillot*, and the one-man chorus in a modern version of *Antigone*.) He had seen too many starving want-to-be actors in New York while he was finishing his doctorate at Columbia University (where his dissertation was the first American translation of de Saussure). Wade was also careful to point out that he had also met starving poets. On the wall of his study was a framed copy of a poem that Maxwell Bodenheim had given him, the one with the passage that reads "the little silver birds of death." Ominous words for one who was torn among three possible professions—poet, actor, critic. I would, of course, try to have the best of it all, by formally completing a Ph.D. in comparative literature at the University of Arkansas, by writing, translating, and publishing poetry, and by writing a critical study of works by Malcolm Lowry and Thomas Mann.

After graduating from SOSU, in the spring of 1964, I married a girl whom I had dated for two years, Cora FloDell McKown. It was not a happy match, though I lied to myself for nearly seven years that it was. There was more than a little professional jealousy involved in the match, since she too was an English major. We stayed together through my years of graduate school and three years of teaching in Tahlequah, at Northeastern State College. With the move to Missouri in 1970 and by the summer of 1972, the marriage was doomed. We were divorced in 1973. You wonder whose fault it all was and, ultimately, have to admit that sometimes two people just cannot be together for very long without friction, regardless of how they may have felt in the beginning.

I was writing poems all through graduate school, at the University of Arkansas. Regardless of the work load of study and the graduate assistantships I held, the writing continued. I began to place pieces in magazines—*Prairie Schooner, Discourse, Nimrod*—and it was only a matter of time before I was classed as one of the contemporary Native American writers, an academic ethnic category given "legitimacy" by Scott Momaday's winning the Pulitzer Prize for *House Made of Dawn* in 1969. That was all right with me, but I have always made it clear that I wanted to be called a writer or a poet because of my work, not because of my blood.

I was married the second time in November 1973, to Carolyn Louise Ahlborn, a native of the town we have made our home in for twenty-one years. It has been a good, solid marriage for both of us. We have two sons (Carolyn's by a first marriage, adopted by me), and I have written over five hundred poems, short stories, and essays. It may not be fair to Carolyn to gauge a relationship by the number of books produced, but she assures me that she approves of such a yardstick.

The Planting

Beside the ash bending
in homage to summer wind,

I will plant the elm, rooted
in the earthen bowl you turned.

The blood-red moon, rising,
will witness my druid's hands,
and what I speak in the night
over grass and stone will long

hold these limbs and roots
together as we have sworn
our love till death. Not from seeds
are these two to live, but from

a felt bond, a breath,
I now make as we ourselves
made promising till death.
And while trees stand, not just

these two, but all, so too we—
within soft hands of each other,
yet free in the summer wind
to rise and fall, touch or not touch—

will stand straight in love's gravity.

In the winter of 1965 I bought a house above the shores of Lake Tenkiller, at Petit Bay, some five or six miles south of Tahlequah, where I was hired to teach introductory English courses. It was not an extraordinary house, but it was perched rather precariously on a hill above the bay. What I remember most about moving in was that first I had to move the spiders and centipedes out. I hired a local exterminator who blasted the house inside and out with malathion, which I discovered much later on was a danger not only to pests but to humans as well. I had never seen a centipede over two or three inches long until I called the exterminator. We measured a bright yellow and black one, slow in dying, to be seventeen inches long. This was wild and woolly country, the western edge of the Cookson Hills.

The house itself was largely wood and glass, with a large room-wide stone fireplace. The roof was cantilevered, with the central beaming running through the chimney and protruding three feet on the outside. The whole south side of the house was, on the main floor, a series of jalousie windows, through which you could get the south wind in summer coming up off the lake. The cedar siding on the house was stained a solid brown. Gray houses were by this time things of my distant past.

From the house downward toward a lake access road ran a stony acre, on which was planted a small vineyard. Also there were great patches of wild blackberry briars, a refuge for the ever-present rattlesnakes and garden-raiding rabbits. I tried half-heartedly to grow a few tomatoes among the grapevines, but finally gave up. The soil was just too stony to hold the nutrients needed for tomatoes. The grapes, however, grew black and plump by fall.

All the summer months, when I was not teaching or in classes at the University of Arkansas, fifty miles away, I was walking the shores of Lake Tenkiller and the hills beyond. The countryside was literally littered with the debris of hundreds of tool-making sites of the ancients. I could never, would never, excavate a site where I found evidence of tool making or of mound burial. On the other hand, I would keep whatever I found on the surface, noting the exact position of the find on a geological survey map for future reference.

As the surface of the lake rose and fell, mostly at the will of the Corps of Engineers, the washline of the lake would eat away the loose dirt and clay to reveal whatever had been covered by the ages. Toward the end of my stay at Petit Bay, in 1968, I had a fifty-five-gallon barrel full of manos and five or six fine metates that I had found at Petit Bay and on around to the north toward Etta Bend. These items, along with hundreds of arrowheads, I hold in trust. I would like for them, in some future sane age, to be scattered back where they belong. But who is to say when that will be?

Looking for Arrowheads

Check the horizon for a rise
that should not be there.

Circle until the sun is in your eyes:
long shadows can tell you the lay of stone or bone.

Keep your eyes hard against the ground:
never turn for the cracked twig,
and know the sky takes care of its own.

Carry a stick grown long enough for prodding:
your vision must be higher than a bent back,
or you will lose the perspective
it takes your life to gain.

Know that shapes are various:
fluted, triangular, rectangular,
sunfished, toothed, blunt,
some without notch or haft,
some hardly touched by human hand.

If you are lucky,
hold the arrowhead in your good right hand,
raise it to the sun,
and give thanks
for the certainty you have come to know
of what may and may not endure.

At one spot, not too far east from the boat dock at Petit
Bay, when the lake was very low because of the drought of
summer, I found a low circle of red rocks and, where the
silt had been washed away by the lake's backing off toward
old river beds, soft white bones. I placed the red rocks back
over the bones, hoping no one would further disturb the
site until the lake rose again. I hope that I prayed for rain.

Two hundred yards or so above the western end of Petit
Bay, one day at the end of summer I stumbled upon a lone
marker where no marker should really have been. The stone
obelisk was scarcely three feet high and very thin. Carved
vertically on it was a date and one word in Cherokee, *child*.

There was no evidence that I could make out of there ever having been a house anywhere within a radius of at least three hundred yards. I could imagine that this was a transient death, perhaps happening just before the end of the long Trail of Tears. More likely, it was the grave of a lost child whose family had lived in a gray boxed house that in time simply rotted away as so many of its kind have over the course of nearly two centuries. There were never foundations for those houses, only stones stacked at the corners and in key places along the side of the house to raise the joists above the moisture of the ground. Those houses were as transient as those of us, Cherokee, Choctaw, or white, who lived in them. I have known people to move from one place to another and take their houses with them, board by board. I have sat in those gray houses in winter, around cane heaters, their stovepipes glowing red from the burning of seasoned hickory wood within, and watched neighbors spit tobacco juice through the cracks between the boards on the floor.

Autobiography, Chapter XIV:
Tombstone at Petit Bay, near Tahlequah

Looking for artifacts that map your world less read,
    you find the obelisk, dwarfed among the weeds;
    knee-high and almost growing from the chert
    hillside, it hides its legend like night the
    features of a face.

You read the date, 1839. And the one faint vertical
    word, *child*, in Sikwayi script. The grave where
    no grave should be gently shocks your senses
    clean: each fracture of chert is bone. You feel
    a sudden reverence for all stone.

Years you've quested in these hills, a running search
   for something still you cannot name—something
   holy, proof of migration or lost Phoenician sailors.

You are tempted toward a gentle excavation, but know
   you will not dig into the earth for the same
   reason you never move the soil except to plant.

The obelisk casts a shadow longer than its length.
   The narrow darkness leans along the hill, toward
   the bay and the slow moon rising from the fabled
   east.

   The house on the hill above Petit Bay was a good place
for writing. It was here that I wrote "The Reapers" and the
first handful of poems that I realized were good enough to
call poems and to submit to magazines I believed in as
organs of fine writing. Perhaps I could have written as well
elsewhere. Perhaps this was the point in time toward which
I had been growing for so many years, the point where I
could distinguish the worth or worthlessness of what I was
writing. At any rate, this was the time that I stopped doing
lots of silly things in my work, such as flagrantly imitating
the recently dead giants of American literature.
   I could sit at the windows on early mornings in the fall
and see, in the distance, deer come down to the lake's edge
to drink. Nearly any night after first frost, I could hear
the yap of coyotes in the hills, and sometimes, if I listened
carefully, I could hear the sound of fox feet in the dry leaves
around the house. It was a lonely time, and a time of much
reflection. I wanted to write stories and poems that would
survive me, and I was very afraid that I would not. Without
knowing it, during this time of reflection, this time of late

beginnings, I was continuing to store up images that would
be with me the rest of my writing days.

Poem on His Birthday

    Under the emptying clouds
by the shaking elms on the broken grade
    where the rapid foxes crowd
his heels, on his rough lawn this day
    in the blinding showers of snow,
this snowbound day in a cloud-bound time,
    he hears no birthday toll
in his frost-haired fifty-ninth year of crime.
    The foxes watch him go

    under the elms and stop
between the pines to lean against
    shrouding shadows that drop
like blankets full of night. The fence
    that's falling down is full
of snow fur half a furlong round
    the humping hill. The lure
of snow on snow that's never loud,
    soft in its white and sure,

    has him or time enthralled.
He walks with foxes at his feet,
    and the foxes on the hill talk
to him through the snow-dreamed
    last afternoon of fall.
The chatter of their say and song
    seems hunter lent, a fox's
years spent in roll and clutch, a psalm
    that only a fool would mock.

Foxes not foxes, but ghosts
of those who were. He walks where they
        had romped when the hill rose
bloomed through the moss-covered decade
        hounding his lost last youth.
In his slow art and tumored head
        runs a tumbling song too
quick to hold and full of quick death.
        Only art can undo

        the tangled life vined off
into the snowy slopes. In his
        fifty-ninth year he ought
not drift afield, he knows, but hit
        a rhythm that will gain
on time's quick wheels. The latest lines
        must run with foxes' fame,
not his, with a foxfire life to outlie
        the moon in wax and wane.

Above Lake Tenkiller, to the north, the Illinois River cuts
a rugged path down from the high country near Siloam
Springs. It is a short but fast river, fed by hundreds of cold
springs, that drops by a series of rapids that are a canoeist's
dream. Bluff burials have been discovered in the limestone
cliffs that line its banks, and evidence of passage and habita-
tion is quite common, especially in projectile points as large
as your hand. From the upper reaches of the Illinois, down
past Tenkiller, south through the San Bois, and on the Winding Stair and Kiamichi mountains, there are places that are
alive with a spirit that informs my world, ancient places
that grip the heart and make it throb with the ache of knowing. No matter how the face of the land changes or how
many tourists I have to step around on my way to them, I

will keep returning. For each time I go back, I feel my being
lifted up by something I know but absolutely cannot name.

The Body Falters

The forest thickens
my blood. I stumble
on acorns grown
the size of apples,
sticks no larger
than the gnat's eye.
I am animal
in this old darkness
I have not known
for years. The body
falters, the mind
joins the earth.
The sound of crawling
cracks my ears
and of the lively trees,
the brown, brown grass,
and the one voice
of the steady river.
I have never been
anywhere but here,
flat on my stomach
embracing the constant
earth, this world
I hold. Sky on my back
I feel the needled wheel
of stars with pores
deep as moonlight.

My eyes break into
the earth, into
the dark alluvial
blood. Beyond
this place:
only another
and another
and another.
I am repeated
into the earth.

To be in Paris is enough, but it is even more special to be there to perform your work. Along with a goodly number of other poet-translators, I was invited to give a reading of some of my poems on November 4, 1991, in the crypt of La Madeleine, a church that traces its origin back to the thirteenth century. I have read my work in some strange places during the past twenty years, but never before have I been scheduled for a crypt. I looked forward to the reading with some keen anticipation, imagining everything from a grandiose setting (such as the crypt of the Pantheon where the sarcophagi of Voltaire and Rousseau are in full view) to a dank wine cellar or the catacombs where one might view the bones of Jean Valjean for a modest fee.

The poetry reading was a spinoff from the Thirteenth Annual Anglo-Français Festival de Poésie, held in June 1990, to which I was an invited participant. What happened before the festival and also during the conference was a mutual translation of poems: English-speaking poets translated French-speaking poets and vice versa. Between classes and on free days at Truman State University during the winter of 1989–90, I spent several weeks translating from six to eight poems for each of the several French poets who were

to participate in the festival. My translating concentrated on
poems by Max Alhau (France), Daniel Biga (France), Fulvio
Caccia (Canada), Nina Cassian (Romania), William Cliff
(Belgium), Hélène Dorion (Canada), Hughes Labrusse
(France), and Sara-Claire Roux (France).

The Festival de Poésie was a bit misleading in title. For
in actuality there was no revelry or rivalry, as one would
expect in the world of Po-Biz today, but instead several days
of brain-breaking retranslation in a sit-down-around-the-
table situation. It turned out to be a true international work-
shop devoted to an exchange of ideas, to the best translation
possible of a number of poets whose work is known beyond
the borders of their own countries. Besides those poets
whose work I was translating, also present were other nota-
ble poets with international reputations: Hilary Davies
(United Kingdom), John Deane (Ireland), Lorand Gaspar
(France), Erin Mouré (United Kingdom), Peter Riley (United
Kingdom), Jacques Rancourt (France), and C. K. Williams
(USA). The beauty of such a festival as this was that you
were face to face with the poets whose work you were
translating, and at the same time you were face to face with
the poets who were translating your work. There was no
rivalry; there was much goodwill expressed on every hand
during the week's festival at the Théatre des Dechargeurs
in the very center of Paris (near Les Halles and the Georges
Pompidou National Center for the Arts and Culture).

At the Festival de Poésie

In a dressing room the size of a closet
in Vicki's theater, we crowd around
the table to translate what cannot be
done. The poems lie about us, scattered
into our lives like sibylline leaves

the Paris wind has thrown. We speak in tongues
not even we are sure of.

                    The day lives
elsewhere. A smoky night fogs our vision:
the rain is fierce in the courtyard beyond
our fanning door. Too many words limp past
our chairs and out into the liquid light.
The poems all deal with broken lives we
try to puzzle out the pieces of.

                        Luck
and the chance word we wish for, a mythy
phrase that will hit our heads like sewer steam
in alleys we dread to walk. Too many
hours we almost it: our minds are growing
dark with poetry.

                If there was but a way
to level out our tumbling tongues, if there
was but a way to say it forever right,
then we would have our paradise in words
and no business whatever in the world.

    In addition to the writers at work at the festival, a number
of other writers stopped by to talk about translating in general or to offer advice. Jean Migrene, who has translated the
poetry of Henry Taylor (a Pulitzer Prize winner a few years
ago) and Richard Wilbur (former poet laureate), graciously
worked with the group for three days. I had first met Jean
in Grenoble in November 1989, where Carolyn and I were
participating in a similar festival devoted to poetry and
translation. He is presently translating some of my work
into French. Also stopping by one day was Charles Juliet,

who is working with Louis Olivier (Grand Valley State University) to translate a group of my poems into French. Charles Juliet's novel *L'année de l'éveil* was the literary event in Paris in 1990. He has long been revered throughout France for his poetry and journals, and now no doubt will be for his fine autobiographical novel.

The director of the festival had also invited several painters to participate in the conference for the purpose of visually illustrating poems from among those being translated. The artwork, from traditional to three-dimensional, added a depth and grandeur that made the festival more than just a literary happening. Among the artists exhibiting were Phan Kim Dien, a Vietnamese whose work is now widely recognized in Europe, and Guerryam, from Grenoble, who is known throughout France for her rock paintings. The acquaintances I made or renewed during that time will have a lasting impact on much of what I write or translate from now on.

Passerelle Debilly

Under the blue awning of the brasserie,
warmed by coffee and the thought of Paris
now washed by November rain, we talk of
things we never dreamed we'd ever get to
see, the awful tower and its lights, love-
making in broad daylight (near Baudelaire's tomb),

no one drunk on wine. The coffee is strong
enough to keep us up all day. All wrong
seems to have left the city. Waves of rain
pound the traffic on Quai Branly into
a funeral march, the engines a slow refrain,
a song that no one now is mourning to.

A certain spirit runs through all of us:
there are days like this in Paris you trust
your life to when nothing can go wrong, not
even rain. The Passerelle is blocks away:
we're wrapped in a coat of rain, warm as it ought
to be. We want the light showers to stay

awhile. The light on the Passerelle, Monet
would see distinctly bright and paint today
indelibly for us on this bridge where
only walkers may go. Blue on more blue
and the rainbowing in of all the glare
and glitter, the golden mosaic hue

of lights on the Seine he would see and paint
a world to see. In this light we grow faint
knowing how short the light is anywhere,
shorter still because we know it is short
and because we are at this moment *here*
where every bridge leads to a royal court.

I do not overestimate the importance of the years 1989
and 1990. I think the development of my work (especially
poetry and fiction) will continue to reflect an international
influence, an influence that was actually begun in my undergraduate days at Southeastern Oklahoma State with the
studies in French and German under Wade Baskin. I am now
at work on a volume of poems set in Europe, mainly Paris.

The spring of 1990 was doubly important to me. Not only
did the festival open up a literary door that had formerly
remained closed, but a Rockefeller Bellagio Study Center
Residency also gave me five uninterrupted weeks in northern Italy in which to translate from the French and German.

Thus I had had an extended period before the 1990 festival
in which to translate, to retranslate, to think, to rest.

Behind much of this literary activity, my home university
stands as a bastion of support. Without its help, its willing-
ness to nurture my art, I would not have gotten to participate
in either the festival or the Bellagio residency. It is gratifying
to know that Truman understands that state and national
boundaries are meaningless anymore in terms of learning
and culture. The day of regionalism and narrow-mindedness
is past. The future of universities, businesses, and individual
careers lies in an international exchange of ideas more than
anything else. That is why I feel language and language
use is so important these days, whether in poetry, literary
translation, or daily speech.

Early in 1991 a few of the results of the Festival Anglo-
Français de Poésie were published in *La Traductière*, the
annual anthology edited by Jacques Rancourt, the director
of the festival. The poems, chosen by Rancourt, were in his
opinion those most difficult to translate and at the same
time those that interested the participants most. One of the
two of my poems included in the publication is a villanelle:

The Game

The mad dog barked because he had to bark
at the dangerous shadows leaping toward his eyes:
we pulled his chain and clamored up the oak

in a fine delicious fear of teeth as sharp
as the spikes of stars spinning atop the trees.
The mad dog barked because he had to bark

at threats he defined as cruelty at the throat.
O, those were the nights we could win any prize:
we pulled his chain and clamored up the oak;

his nose objecting to our heels, his joke
not quite the same as our own, but surely close.
The mad dog barked because he had to bark

and play the game his captors chose, but spoke
his words his way, a merry rage set loose:
we pulled his chain and clamored up the oak.

We loved that fierce beast and the deadly stroke
his paws gave our dogged legs and skinned knees.
The mad dog barked because he had to bark:
we pulled his chain and clamored up the oak.

One of the sticking points (there were others such as *rage*, which means "rabid" in French) for my translators was the word *clamored*. To clamor is to exclaim noisely, but in the poem the verb also suggests climbing. Such is the nature of language, often without entire regard to dictionary meaning. For at the heart of translation lies a mutual exchange of ideas, an investigation of life's little or large perplexities, a mutual search for Truth and Beauty and Virtue, the humanity within. Translation has nothing to do with mere transmission of fact.

Now, a year and a half after the Thirteenth Annual Anglo-Français Festival, under a heavy Paris sky with a cold wind off the Seine, Carolyn and I, fortified by an *expresse* at the Café de Peny across the plaza, dutifully made our way to the crypt of La Madeleine. Although we were a few minutes early, I began to doubt we had found the right entrance, though the sign clearly read CRYPT. Several others joined us. Someone was late: the door was still locked. Perhaps a half hour after the scheduled time, a kindly French matron led us around the church to the opposite side, where the reading, she explained, was to be held in the room reserved for cultural events and they were waiting for us. When I asked why we were told the reading was to be in the crypt, she answered that they were sure we could find the crypt. Good French logic, of course: American writers can find their way to the chambers of the dead but not to cultural events. Let us hope that we can change this view.

Of the original festival group, C. K. Williams and I represented the United States. From England, Ireland, and Canada were Hélène Dorion, Hilary Davies, Fulvio Caccia, John Deane, and Peter Riley. The French poets were Max Alhau, Sara-Claire Roux, Hughes Labrusse, and Jacques Rancourt. William Cliff (Belgium) was also present. It was a long reading session, with each poet reading at least three and as many as six of his original works. In the case of the American poets, French translations were also read. The room, though reserved for cultural events, was very like a crypt, long and narrow and low and vaulted. You could well imagine Edgar Allan Poe reading here, or just as darkly, Baudelaire. There were perhaps a hundred people packed into an attentive audience that never wavered in its devotion to poetry throughout the two-and-a-half-hour reading. Hurrah for the good French people and their love of poetry! We are lucky in the Midwest to have a dozen in attendance at a poetry reading by a leading American writer. For my part, I read the two poems Jacques Rancourt included in *La Traductière*, plus two others that had been translated by Charles Juliet and Louis Olivier. French versions of my poems were read by Hughes Labrusse, Sara-Claire Roux, and William Cliff.

One O'Clock in the Morning

On Boulevard Edgar Quinet at one o'clock
in the morning, I thought I saw Poe standing

against the wall, hunched against late traffic.
The graveyard beyond was radiating

light. I could swear he was writing poems
there among the shadows as last bars closed
and the night began to take on final form.
I heard him utter something about a rose,

a rune, a moon, as wild as Baudelaire.
Of course he was dressed in black, the cape
fitting him like a shroud. Translated there
by some twist of ghostdom, he leaned on fate

and honed away on words I hardly heard.
I was close enough to see bad teeth and smell
his wormwood breath. I did not speak. The birds
clattered in the limbs above at the sound of bells

a church or two away. He was gone before
the tone had died, scribbling down the boulevard
away from Montparnasse. At one in the morning
I can't be sure, but I think he walked right through

the traffic, across Raspail, heading up toward
Val du Grace or God knows where, leaving behind
him a penance in sound for the late lords
of poetry, who missed him in his time.

Immediately after the close of the 1990 festival, I read at
the Pompidou Center, on the same program as a poet from
Cuba, one from Canada, and one from Spain, and therefore
was introduced to the French love of cultural events well
in advance of the Madeleine reading. The importance of
international cultural exchange is becoming more evident

each day, and events such as the Madeleine gathering of poets is one of the ways we the poets, the translators, can reach a wider audience and hopefully continue to proclaim the importance of the arts in all our lives. The love of art is a civilizing passion. It was never the politician, the general, or the teacher who was the true nurturer of that thing we call civilization. The fostering parent of civilization is the artist. If we forget the arts, we are doomed to a very dull and deadly life. The importance of the arts lies in the transmission (translation) of ideas and the innovation that almost always comes with such a transmission, in the preservation of tradition, and in the establishing of new traditions. In the arts it is important, as it is in all education, to differentiate between what is fad and what is fabulous. What is fabulous is mythic, and myth as patterns of human existence is what we base our lives on. And poetry is the voice of myth.

Walking Paris is what Carolyn and I like to do most in that great city. In November 1991, when I was just beginning the manuscript of poetry that I now call unabashedly *Paris*, we took our first walk through Père Lachaise, the city's oldest cemetery. Leaves of the plane trees littered the central cobbled avenue, and the narrow streets of the dead were layered with them under the low November sun and clouds. Carolyn and I were looking for Chopin's tomb but had neglected to get a map from the tourist shop by the Ménilmontant gate. We could not see any system to the numbering of the sections of the cemetery. For example, section 5 lay next to 73, Carolyn pointed out, shaking her head. She buttoned the top of her long black leather coat. There was more than a promise of frost in the air. We had been out most of the day, first to Sacré Coeur and now Père Lachaise. We were tired and chilled and walked on without knowing where to look. There was no one about for me to ask in my small French.

At an intersection halfway up the hill, we saw a young couple coming toward us. Pulling our coats a bit tighter about us, we waited as the couple approached. I asked, "Connaissez-vous le tombeau de Chopin?"

"Pardon me?" the girl said. Of course, she was an American, they were both Americans, and very young but obviously mature, more so than her companion, who hid behind his cigarette. Both were dressed in faded jeans, with frazzled rips at the knees, and brown leather jackets. Their hair was dyed red and moussed.

We kept our smiles to ourselves, but I managed a straight face to ask, in English, "Do you know where Chopin's grave is?"

"No, I'm sorry. We're looking for Jim Morrison. We think he's around here somewhere. Do you know?"

We said, no, we were sorry, too, and walked on. We remembered Jim Morrison, or rather, the Doors, and that Morrison had died in Paris and that there was a cult growing out of his adoration.

Finding Oscar Wilde

After the riot in Père Lachaise, streams
of teenage tourists flood the gates. Shadows
of the plane trees gray their faces. It seems
as if they want to mourn but cannot go
beyond the nervous laughter of rock dreams
and Coca-Cola days. Few drink nouveau
Beaujolais now: it's just not chic enough.
Two green-haired girls smoke Gitanes and act tough.

We see two others writing *Morrison*
lives beneath Balzac, in chalk. Our map takes
us past more famous lines and past the sun,
where we pause to grab our breath and then shake
the summer sweat from our hair. Somewhere down
the hill, Abélard and Héloïse wake
again to try to free themselves from the stone
bed they have lain in centuries too long.

All Paris is stone, and there are those graves
everywhere as lonely as Oscar Wilde's
broad tomb. Rioting Morrison fans behaved
as a herd behaves, coming in droves to mill
round redundancy. No solitaire to save
the senseless crowd the agony of hell
showed up. There will never be a crowd round
the other slab where Oscar Wilde kneels down,

the tall wings booked by his writing hand.
Nor need there be. The legend of his life
is not his work. The work, the art, remains.
We lean relaxed upon his stone. At five
we hear the whistles blow for our return,
a prelude to the closing gates and evening
song of sparrows. Leaving we touch a fast
farewell to his high brow and what may last.

As we continued the search for Chopin, we began to notice
a chalked inscription appearing here and there on the stones.
We read: *Jim Morrison lives!* We saw it by Rossini's tomb,
where the roses were fresh. We saw it next to Fauré's grave.
We saw it on the smooth dark face of Colette's stone.

Near the summit of the cemetery, we met two ancient
Parisians. They were arguing about the Bicentennial, as best I
could tell. I stopped them, apologetically, with a half gesture.

"Messieurs, où est le tombeau de Chopin? Connaissez-le?"

"Ah, oui! Là-bas, la deuxième, à gauche."

"A gauche?"

"Oui, à gauche."

"Merci beaucoup, messieurs."

We turned back down the hill.

"Down and to the left. The second path," I said. "Look,
There should be flowers."

Carolyn wanted to be sure about *gauche*.

"*Gauche* is right or left?"

"Left."

"*A gauche*," she said. She was learning French. She repeated the phrase several times, motioning slightly with her left hand at each utterance.

We saw the mourner before we saw the tomb. A woman was standing in the middle of the walk. She was not weeping but was obviously very sad at Chopin's tomb. She was young, although there were lines out from her eyes and the corners of her mouth. She had long thin hands. They were clasped together, loosely holding a crucifix.

The yellow leaves were so thick on the walk that we made no sound as we passed behind the mourner. We stopped a respectable distance from her. We did not want to intrude on the thoughts of another. Carolyn gently squeezed my arm. There was a cascade of white flowers from the feet of the stone muse to the base of the tomb.

"You can smell them from here," Carolyn whispered.

We walked on down the blanket of fallen leaves. We remained very quiet until we were near the wall of the cemetery and were aware of the cold again and of the certainty of rain.

Lovers, Light, November Rain

The November rain swells the Seine
and forces most lovers inside.
Only true lovers stand and strain
in damp doorways against the night.

We know all manner of things ride
the heavy wind. We walk the same
streets anyway. We can't stay mad
that November rain swells the Seine

into flood. Fog helps keep us sane.
The warmth of our bodies abides,
regardless of the autumn rain
that forces most lovers inside.

Of all the artists who have tried
in love and failed and know the pain
that comes with low November light,
only true lovers stand the strain

of loss, lovers who want to claim
as their own all the light outside
that Paris every autumn frames
in damp doorways against the night.

We will never say light has died,
though it limps down the streets, lame
for only as long as lovers lie
wrapped in themselves or whisper names
in the November rain.

The Pini Car Company chauffeur picked us up at the Milano airport in a black Mercedes. It was our first trip to Italy. (There would be others, to Florence and Rome.) The Bellagio residency that I had applied for was now granted, and we were being driven by a diminutive black-suited chauffeur to the Villa Serbelloni for a five-week stay. The Rockefeller Foundation treats its Bellagio artists and scholars as royalty, I had been told, and now we were to witness it all firsthand.

Spring was flourishing everywhere, in the gardens of Milan, the fields outside the city, and along the shore of Lake Lecco. We were riding north across some two thousand years of civilization, taking roads that had been taken before by soldier, philosopher, poet, seeing shapes of field, valley, mountain that had been seen before by tens of thousands of travelers who loved and hated or built and destroyed the country we call Italy.

Villa after villa passed before our eyes, the azaleas and rhododendrons brilliant in the late afternoon sun. Vista after vista held our gaze. So many flowers in a country where every view was a picture postcard you could dream into. How a land so vibrant in color, so rich in humanity could have been so ravished, so virginal, so strong, so weak down

through the centuries is still the subject for artist and
scholar alike.

   And then along Lake Como: Villa Giulia, Villa Melzi, Villa
Carlotta, Villa Serbelloni—magical names, each with its own
hint of fame or infamy, each with its own particular style,
and each with its own garden of earthly delights. The last
ten miles, the road was so narrow that there was no center
line. We had not imagined a land of such astonishing beauty
and contrast. Carolyn was immediately in love with landscape and I also. But more than that, the knowing that you
were walking the ground where Dante had walked, where
Pliny the Younger had built his Villa Tragedia, where Liszt
had composed, where Stendhal had written, where countless
great and lesser men and women had taken the time to
create something of value out of and for this world. There
is, also, the other: the records of failure, of loss, of evil: the
slaughter of innocents, the reign of tyrants, the government
of fools. The mind is in constant dance in such a region.

May 1990, Tremezzo, Where Mussolini Died

"Villa Carlotta where Mussolini died,"
your tour guide speaks, among the roses and bells,
to a Nippon history buff whose Nikon levels
on the villa's azaleas on each side

of the brilliant terraces. Il Duce lied
to them in Rome and ran for the villa
and Fascist friends, ran to merchants in silk,
lords who promised him Switzerland. You fight

the urge to strangle the guide and make him get
facts right. Tremezzo two hundred yards away
shuts down for lunch. The long Italian noon

blanches stone walls where yesterday you met
his ghost arm in arm with Sophia Loren's gray
sister, Claire, who, with her slender free hand,

carefully held her dress down against the wind,
against the dance of dust where all love ends.

Bellagio sits on the eastern shore of Lake Como below the
high hill that is the promontory separating the two lakes. It
is a town steeped in history, all residents are quick to admit.
Mussolini and his girlfriend were shot just across the lake
and strung up like beeves by the partisans. Longfellow
stayed awhile very near the same spot, in Hotel Bellevue.
Everywhere you turn there is a plaque honoring the residency of someone you know and someone you don't. As
a Rockefeller resident, you, too, are honored: 10 percent
discount at all shops. As you open the gate (above one of
the busy, narrow streets) to the Villa Serbelloni grounds and
step down into the flow of pedestrians, you are by virtue
of your place on the hill the lord and lady of the manor.

Shopping in Bellagio is precarious: you can fall into debt
with a single purchase. Two hundred thousand lire for a
hand-knit sweater! Eighty-six thousand lire for a ceramic
mask of Pan! "These are weekend prices," one shop owner
told me. "We get lots of Saturday sailors from Milan, you
know. For you, I will negotiate." The Milan sailors (silk
merchants and their set) probably know better than to shop
Bellagio. It is a tourist town, with tourist prices, regardless
of the Rockefeller discount. Even a mixed-blood from Oklahoma can tell that. The prices, however, do not take away
the fact of the excellent art and workmanship of nearly
everything the shops have for sale. No merchant could call
Bellagio home and have bad taste. The sky, the water, the
mountains forbid it.

Francesca e Paolo: Bellagio

A jewelry store with everything my wife
imagines golden about Lombardy. Of course,
we go in, past cheap coral and a horse
on a plastic pedestal. The lovely life

of Dante's airborne sinful lovers lifts
our eyes, lusty flesh tones some painter forced
out of black velvet. All the junk we swore
we would avoid draws us in as if

we have no will against the dime-store lures
glittering under glass. Outside, the ferry
sounds its horn, and Charon draws the gangplank

in, the passengers for Tremezzo sure
they will reach Villa Carlotta. I say
we are just looking, and fee! my Italian sink

as the pale proprietress insists we hold
the bookmark she tells us is pure spun gold.

The few weeks we spent in residence at the Villa Serbelloni
were given largely to work and relaxation. Work consisted
mainly in translating, from German, Dagmar Nick's *Gezählte
Tage* (Numbered days), a torturous task because of her precise imagery and infusion of Teutonic and Greek myth. In
the German the poems are crystalline in their purity of sound
and sense. Thus the torturous problem in translation: how
to reflect that in another language and at the same time
remain true to the German. Of course, on a slightly different
level, the same thing is true of all writing: how to reflect
image or idea in language. By the end of the five weeks at

Villa Serbelloni I had translated (and in several instances retranslated my translations) about half of the poems in the volume and was able to give a few days to my own work, making an initial effort on a group of poems that would become the final section of *The Sawdust War*.

Many were the walks Carolyn and I took on the fifty-acre Serbelloni estate, which was willed to the Rockefeller Foundation by the heiress ("The Princess") of the Hiriam Walker Cooperation on the condition that it be administered as a residence for artists and scholars. The grounds themselves bear traces of culture that date to at least the first millennium before Christ.

In Another Country

With my hands I scoop the deep stone bowl free
of muck the trees and wind have deposited
over the years. Strange to find a Celtic
metate worn down by grinding so deep

so far above the lake and old grain fields.
A low stele of granite, a stile, a nick
in time, this bowl, this horn of plenty, has fed
the multitudes. Strange, too, to think what zeal

they must have had to bring the grain this far
for grinding. More than a simple stone, it was
a sacrament long before the Romans

came to build a tower on the hill. The dark
stone speaks of loss. In another country, I push
aside the leaves, and my own loss begins

to fade: the song I make is a poor offering
beside this stone. I should bring gold and grain.

   Near the top of the promontory hill, on a path leading
up to the ruins of a castle dating from the fourth century,
is a cement bust of Pliny with the inscription

HIC TRAGEDIA

MARCVS PLINIVS IVNIOR

honoring the man of letters whose villa stood on the same
spot as the present Villa Serbelloni, halfway up the hill. You
stop to wonder, if you know Pliny the Younger's work, how
many letters to Tacitus Pliny may have written from this
spot. And a few yards farther up lie the ruins of a stone
foundation of a Roman tower erected before the time of
Octavian. You cannot but wonder here at the course of
things. Why, for example, the medieval castle atop the promontory? Its ruins show walls six feet thick. The obvious
reason is a lookout over the Lecco arm of the lake and the
northern approaches. More likely, however, the promontory
was under constant siege. Celt, Gaul, Lombard—all were
fierce in determination against the rule of Rome.

Castle Keep

Three hundred feet above the lake, the fort
is turning back from stone to soil. The high
wall crumbles daily onto the grass by
the retaining wall we sit on to court

the destiny we read on wings that sort
the wind below into messages cried
by gulls. White against the black lake they fly
infinite figure eights below the fort,

guarding their nests on the sheer cliff's face.
We hear the wind beneath and other sounds
we cannot identify. Something chthonian

is tunneling into our lives. This place
takes hold of us and draws our eyes around
precipitous ways. The risks that we take on

climbs would made a sane man dizzy. We run
the trails that lead us to more than ruins.

If you are in residence, you cannot stay off the lake for very long. Something about it calls you, something deep and primeval. It is a glacial lake formed and sustained by snowmelt from both Italian and Swiss Alps. Over a thousand feet deep in places, it is the mirrored half of the Alps above it. On the lake, you feel the slide of ice about you, the tumbling down of stone, the last echo of earthquake. but you row through and into a knowledge of water that no tourist can perceive. Even though you have not rowed in forty years, you are tempted on days when the wind is down, or blowing lightly from the west, to row down the glazed surface of the lake and know the mystery of voyage. It does not take you long, however, to realize that on most afternoons in the spring and early summer the wind will change and start coming up from the south, gently at first, then sometimes with a whitecapping will that is unbearable for most small boats.

Carolyn and I were caught on the lake in the Serbelloni dinghy when the wind changed to blow straight and hard out of the south, up the Lecco arm. We had set out at ten in the morning to row to Villa Giulia a mile down the lake and had in fact rowed out from the Villa's dock several hundred yards toward the middle of the lake. Without warning, the wind was suddenly from the south, and the stern of the little boat was being slapped by two-foot waves every three seconds. The sky fell like a thrown blanket on boat and shore.

South Wind

The day we row to Villa Giulia
starts clear and calm, the surface of the lake
smooth and green. Café terraces in the wake
of the dinghy fall away soft as villa

songs wafting out from Pescallo. No Scylla
lurks beneath and no sirens curse the lake
this early in the day, though we know a late
wind always comes up from the south, a killer

for small boats. But light turns heavy with clouds
before we reach the villa's dock, and the wind
picks up force early and makes me pull the oars

hard. The day grows dark, a nasty shroud
of rain covers us, and the lake and rain
become one mass. We are blind to the shore

we may never touch again. Nothing to do
but go with the wind that has our boat in tow.

We were at that moment Hemingway's Catherine and Frederick, and "I kept on rowing, until suddenly we were close ashore against a point of rock that rose beside us; the waves striking against it, rushing high up, then falling back. I pulled hard on the right oar and backed water with the other and we went out into the lake again." I had to put my entire body to the chore of keeping the stern to the hard south wind, which would take us back to the boathouse, if we were lucky, before the storm broke upon us.

Beyond the walls of the villa grounds, trails snake up and down the hills. Most of them are of ancient origin, medieval in their concept of road, bedded with pebbles from stream and glacial flow, and most often they are walled. Often as you walk along, your legs bending groaningly upward in the climb, you sense the presence of time past. There are ways of the wind that take hold of you, smells that tell you this is another world, sounds you cannot identify.

Mule Track to Suira

Last days in Bellagio and we want to walk
the cobbled paths the Lombards call mule tracks.
For us, hard trails. From Pescallo we take
the walled trails and groan upward. We can't talk:

Lake Como air is lead and fog. The chalky
walls sweat, and the green vineyards beyond sag
with blooms. At Villa Belmonte we shake
the sweat from our hair, panting and balking

at the steep climb for the sake of climb we set
ourselves upon. Above the fog the track
levels out. We walk easily along the crest

down through Aureggio, the smell of bread
surrounding us and the sun upon our backs,
then turn upward again, toward Suira, past

a hill garden and an old woman who waves
at us for love of garlic or strange faces.

Beginning at Villa Giulia, there is a broad swath, two
hundred yards in width, that has been graded level for a
quarter of a mile to the shore of the Como arm of the lake
at Loppia. A seventeenth-century lord of the villa had his
will: to be able to wake mornings and see both the eastern-
most and westernmost shores of the lake. The immediate
effect on the visitor is that here is a grand playing field, as
indeed it was, once dotted with pavilions, peopled with
aristocrats from all the great villas along the lake. The im-
mensity of the former wealth and grandeur of Villa Giulia
is staggering. What suffering labor it must have taken to
level the hills between the two arms of the lake and what
audacity to order it are, even now at the end of the twentieth
century, still familiar traits of this thing we call civilization.
The walled trails above the allée seem to suffer themselves
endlessly the long way around to anywhere. In contrast,
they seem ancient and far more mysterious than the flat
atrocity below them.

To Loppia

Leaving Suira and the hard climb from Villa
Giulia's broad allée that cuts across
to Loppia as level as the lake, we are lost
in a maze of walled trails and the tropical

plants that cannot be there but are: the hill
is home to a forest thick with Spanish moss
and palms. We gauge the stone trail by fossils
too strange for this world and find it is still

the same hard road it has always been. The red
roofs of Loppia come into view. The long
lake boats, like a gypsy caravan at a fair,

are decked with silk from Como or fish, lead
sinkers and nets hanging from their prows. A song,
oddly Streisand, hangs on the morning air,

and we know this too is Lombardy, where
the bells can ring familiar at any hour.

The gardens of the Villa Melzi stretch along the lake shore
from Loppia to Bellagio, a mile or more of riotous red and
white and purple and pink in April and May when the
rhododendrons and azaleas are in bloom. Cypress trees
grow in the edge of the lake, their perpetual mourning coun-
terpointed by the uncontrolled joy of flowers. Here and there
a gnarled pine will remind you of what it takes to stand
firm in a country that has known as much change as northern
Italy. It is a garden where formality runs wild. There is a
Japanese vista here, a labyrinth of vine there, a geometrical
boxwood hedge, a sculpted tree, and the melodic blackbirds
everywhere. The hardest of hearts would melt in this grand
liberty of light.

There was nothing more soothing than our walks through
the Melzi Gardens. The paths were smooth, and there were
no hills to climb, no ledges to step up. The level paths
meandered happily along the lovely lawn which merged
with the water's edge.

In the Melzi Gardens

On the shore of Lake Como, looking westward,
Dante leans toward his Beatrice. In white
stone they are frozen in the midst of bright
azaleas. The warm spring sun has lured

us down from the Villa Serbelloni, the lords
of discipline having left us late last night.
How hard it is to write, even though you might
enjoy a fellowship, with the ghosts of bored

artists hovering about this pavilion.
We would like to reach the absolute in art,
the meaning behind the flowers and the stones,

a labyrinth that nearly takes our own
concept of paradise away with the riot
of rhododendrons and Dante's face grown

soft with love. Here in the Melzi Gardens
we look for light that will let our words go on.

In contrast, the gardens—there are several—of Villa Serbelloni are quite small, the most important of which are the
terraces up the face of the hill to the villa itself. Each terrace
is in itself a miniature formal garden characterized by boxwood hedges, among which are clusters and beds of every
kind of flower from early tulip to late rose. The smell of
oleander, the balm of Gilead, and the ever-present boxwood
permeates the hillside. Conical, spherical, and rectangular
evergreens take your eyes at every turn. Everything is in its
place, bordered in green and accentuated by primary colors.
    During our five-week Bellagio residency, we lived in *la
Maranese*, just two terraces down from the villa, a small
complex of four apartments. Daily, we took our meals at
the main house, walking up past the cherry trees laden with
fruit and down the manicured terraces three times a day.
We never tired of going through the gardens, often stopping
at a bench to contemplate the odors or the magnificent views
of both the Lecco and Como arms of the lake. There were

days we could see forever, so clear it was. But there were those days quite the contrary, with fog and mist draping the hill so that you could not even see the olive orchard or the Frati down below. Once we stopped by the princess's little dog's tomb and sat for a few minutes inside the box-wood enclosure, the size of the log cabin I helped build on Nanny Ridge all those years ago. A tiny tombstone read "Wurstl." We were sad for a few moments, but then the sun called us back to the other things of the garden and we rejoiced in our good fortune of being there.

In the Formal Garden

The little dog lies in the boxwood tomb
the late princess had the gardeners frame
over his grave. You can step in anytime,
sit and contemplate in the cool, clipped room

a dog's life or your own. By this green home
the small shrubs take on shapes that seem to climb
the hill. Their leafy ears and noses mime
daily unfailing greetings as they come

to cluster round His Majesty. No call
from master, mistress, or slave can sway them from
their devotion. The terrace is fresh with

roses, and if dogs have ghosts, then Wurstl
would never want to leave. I think the balm
of Gilead alone would hold me to this

garden and the Villa Serbelloni if
I were to end here, my tomb on the cliff.

Near the foot of the promontory hill, at the lower edge
of the olive orchard, stands the Frati. During our stay at the
Villa, the Rockefeller Foundation was finally completing a
long project of renovating the monastery, called by the local
people the Frati (after the monks who in former times
worked the grounds). It was established in the seventeenth
century by the lord who then owned the estate, one Sfondrati. The story goes that he was an evil lord, inflicting
innumerable injustices upon his people. He was, however,
devoted to his son, who, it seems, wanted to become a priest.
In order to keep his son on the estate and yet satisfy the
son's yearning, Sfondrati built the monastery and brought
in priests and monks and saw his son eventually ordained
in all the church's splendor. The monastery was kept going
by successive owners down through the centuries. Most of
the monks were buried on the east side of the hill on the
cliff facing the rising sun. The graveyard is now at the bottom
of the Lecco arm of Lake Como, having broken free from
the main cliff several years ago. The civic authorities dyna-
mited the cemetery into the lake because it was "a threat
to navigation." Twelve monks are buried in the crypt in
the Frati.

We did not visit the monastery until two days before we
finished our residency. It seemed a dreary place in spite of
the renovation, with cell after cell for the monks who from
daylight to dark must have farmed the garden terraces and
the orchard and who most likely had most of the household
chores in the villa to do. The one bright spot of the Frati,
however, was the chapel. Its walls were vivid in new white
paint, and the way the diffused light filtered through the
high windows gave off an atmosphere of high and holy
reverence. To sit on the sturdy oak pews was to feel yourself,
however remotely, a part of all that the Frati had been.

A small group of the residents had come down with Peter
Platt, a composer from Australia, to see his studio, which

was in the Frati. He also wanted us to see the chapel and
hear how well it complimented the sound of music. I have
never heard anything quite so awe-inspiring as the sound
of Peter's oboe in the stillness of the Frati at sundown. When
Arthur Loeb, the director of the Carpenter Center at Har-
vard, joined Peter, the medieval music and song they made
transported us into that older age of the grotesque and
the sublime.

The Frati: Crypt, Chapel, Oboe

below the Villa Serbelloni
for Peter and Jean Platt

The courtyard is full of sun and weeds. Stone
gives way to grass. Silence spreads down
the colonnade as fast as shadows of clouds.
Each door is a station of the cross, although
now no brothers pray in cells, no brothers go
forth at dawn to work the villa. The drone
of traffic in Bellagio gives way to the bells
of San Giacomo down the hill. At noon the tone
is definitely Lombard, as mournful
as the plague, ringing of medieval death.
A death's-head marks the only unlocked door.
Behind it shadow is a constant shroud, the floor

dry with ash someone tried to teach a lesson
with, or to clean the stone. A dozen tombs
and just one bears an epitaph: *Pellegrino*
da Lecco in charcoal. And underneath, a skull
and crossed bones in char. Above in white quiet,
Peter Platt, full of song lines, changes a dull
reed, then strokes his oboe into music
for God, long absent from this empty house.

The chapel quivers with tones bounding off
its rejuvenated walls. The wooden mouse-
gnawed cross fills one wall, and the air is thick
with motes of paint and dry rot drifting softly

through the oboe's sacred songs. Peter plays
for all the walls, and the walls play back.
Peter plays, and God comes down and sits on
the front-row pew and sings a chorus, mourns
the Frati gone and even Sfondrati's lost son
who became a priest to expiate the black
sins of the father. Then God sings other
worlds equally sweet and far. Not God, but Peter's
oboe's songs, winged down under holy words
bringing into this lifted fallen house hope,
rendering through reed and simple wood a mood
such as no sermon alone could ever do.

    Down below, on the level space between orchard and boat house, Justin Kaplan and Anne Bernays were warming up for the daily afternoon game of bocci. We took the path winding down through the orchard from the Frati and joined them for one last game of bocci. Anne had amazing control and, as she claimed, a secret wrist action that did the trick. I could never get the hang of the game. To me it was merely shuffleboard, which I have always despised, with balls. Carolyn, however, became quite good at the game and spent many of the afternoons at bocci with Anne and Justin and Charles and Holly Wright. Often, from my study in la Maranese, where I was translating Nick or the French poets, I could hear the click-click of the hard clay balls as they bounced off each other and occasionally a loud cheer from the participants. Beyond the bocci court were the retaining wall at lake's edge, boathouse, gun-gray lake itself and mountains backing it, and always the melodious song of blackbirds.

The black Mercedes came for us at six in the morning. We had packed silently after dinner the night before, and in the dark dawn and mist of the final hours there still were no words. There was nothing that we could say to lift the sadness of the leaving from us. In our minds we were exiles. We could not even think of return until the millennium turned. Ten years, and then there was only the possibility of return, not the return itself. All would depend on the course of my work and its worth in the eyes of others. We could, of course, return to Bellagio whenever we wished. But that would not be the same as a return to the Villa Serbelloni, where every pebble is a bone and every leaf a ghost.

In the early morning air we could hear Peggy, Gianna Celli's Airedale, chasing lizards on the hill above la Maranese, her nose in the cracks of rocks as she exclaimed in subdued *woof-woofs*. The blackbirds had begun their morning songs. Soon we would be gone. In a matter of days, or of hours, others would arrive to claim our place. But a part of us would always remain here on the hill above the olive orchard from where the blackbirds welcomed us each day.

Regatta

For weeks we have lived among the ghosts of gone
writers, artists, historians, scholars
of all sorts. We can hear them at the doors
of the library, the floor creaking, a blown

curtain rising from no wind where the lonely
princess died. The Villa Serbelloni flowers
bloom for all of them. In only hours
now we too will leave the beautiful lawn,

forest, cliff, and looking back will dream
only a ghost of the paradise we knew.
We will see shades of ourselves walking there,

down through the olive orchard, across the stream
the trail becomes in rain, to Pescallo to
watch the regatta set all the white sails for

Varenna, where the right wind blows. We will
remember this even though our minds grow still.

    The road back to Milan was uneventful and dulled by the
oppressive clouds and by the heaviness of farewell that hung
palpably about us. In the hour of departure there was a
wash of gray over everything—the sky, the lake, the hills,
the houses. There was no promise of sun this morning, only
a curtain of mist that would envelope in its folds that which
for us had been. We exchanged no more than a dozen words
on the way to Milan. The sense of severance was so great
that we would have wept if we had tried to talk. We knew
that we would be depressed for days and that not even Paris
would cheer away the loss of this paradise.

In contrast to the tranquility of Bellagio, Paris was with few exceptions pure noise. Nearly everywhere we turned was traffic, either human or machine. We found ourselves seeking out quiet spots—the back streets off St. Germain, Parc Monceau, Père Lachaise. Even the Thirteenth Annual Franco-Anglais Festival de Poésie was loud with the good-natured and garrulous voices of participants, the poets and artists. It took us days to adjust to the constant issuing of sound. But our growing love for the city carried us into a mode we have never shifted out of since that visit. We had been in Paris the year before and would continue to visit the city once or twice each year up to the present time. My grounding in French literature and culture and Carolyn's love for art and high fashion still keep us going back when others want to explore new territories.

After the festival, in 1990, we knew we were hooked on Paris. Carolyn began reading Simone de Beauvoir in 1991 in Hôtel Plaza Haussmann, just up the street a few blocks from Proust's apartment (112 boulevard Haussmann), where for nine years he wrote most of his great novel.

Near Proust's Apartment

No plaque was there to tell us that
you had sat in the little square
late at night when the pollen hid
in the tulip trees. It was there
you rested from the bed, your hat

pulled low, the collar up, and thought
of friends dancing at your expense
in the dusty hall you'd never see
again. Marcel, we did a dance
for you along the gravel walk

to the Chapelle Expiatoire.
Forgive us, please, we did not pray,
but sat awhile beneath the trees
and listened to a late night choir
echoing off rue Pasquier.

Under the evening light we saw
a young tomato vine growing
by the walk's edge where none should be.
We thought of our own gardening,
felt cold memory began to thaw,

something happening in the blood
we wanted to give you credit for.
And in that moment we knew well
that you were right: the budding core
of memory depends upon a mood.

Every night of our stay in Paris we would read a portion
of Simone de Beauvoir's *Prime of Life*. What held us to her

work was the same thing that had held us in the States: the way she could write about anything at all that crossed her mind and never really be off her initial subject. Those long flowing sentences of description of the walks she and Sartre had taken in Bavaria or the south of France that never seemed to end and the sheer majesty of her love for narrative were what we prized in her work. And then there was her absolute committment to the art of writing. Nothing else mattered more.

Upstairs at Café de Flore

A director and a writer (Lanzmann and Bost)
in the corner booth, an oriental
student near the door, and the two of us
well into our *salade verte*. The air vent
beneath our feet hums a slow winter hymn
and cools the streets and stress of summer

we know well. Below, all tables are taken:
the terrace is heavy with thighs and talk
that we are glad to be out of. We shake
our heads in disbelief of ghosts. We thought
the August heat had emptied all cafés.
We are glad to sit beneath vague faces,

crowed scenes framed on the wall, old friends
in this rare atmosphere. *Simone et Sartre,*
we hear from the corner booth, the movie men
easing out of their conversation toward
the stairs. Simone stays with us and smokes
a filter tip. Sartre begins to choke

the student on philosophy that he
himself could never get quite right except
on stage, of which all of Paris was. Free
of the shackles of time, Dali's pursed lips
float up. *Café?* and the waiter pauses.
Simone nods. Sartre lights a blue Gauloise.

Across rue St. Benoit, on the *premier,*
a woman undresses at her window.
We keep watch unabashed, which is to say
another moment is framed against the flow.
Sartre winks across the table and then
lifts his glass of Scotch. Simone fills her pen.

I knew my own work could never be as rich as hers, but
I read her without envy and listened carefully as Carolyn
read sections of the work to me.

It was good to be in Paris, always, and to read the work
of one who knew and loved the city as well as anyone could
in recent years when things had begun to turn bad, when
the art of fiction and poetry had given way to self-absorption.
We were sad that we had not known Simone and Sartre. If
we had just been able to have traveled to Paris a decade or
so earlier, we might have known them. In this way we
mused of what we had missed, and at the same time we
felt that we were a part of something that would affect the
course of history. You cannot be in Paris for any real length
of time without feeling that you are in the flow of things.

By the Seine, a Promise

Paris from Montreuil to Étoile
takes us into a realm we dreamed
wrong for years. Now for a long while
we have come to know the red seams
of the city: the guts, the mean

streets and alleys. The sense of time
lost is almost like some slow game

we are forced to play catch-up in
and will never be winners of.
We come here for lives to begin,
the promise of art and the art of love
that we forget more of each move
we make away from what we once,
young, knew was real. The guilt for months

that will not go away: we kill
the chance to find a way, to get
past the no entry line, or kill
the urge to do what no one yet
has done. We are the real, the bet
we wagered on and thought we lost.
We let the best things slip by most

days. But now at sundown and by
the stream that makes its way past lives
that never see its flow, we try
to say it right. We want to give
our eyes a chance to blink and have
the time to know we're living on
the outer edge of dark. Toward the moon

over Père Lachaise, night birds loop
and cry, their lamentations shrill
as marbles dropped on stone. The hope
of thousands buried there is still
echoed in the falling wind. We will
remember promises and fold
each moment here in the sunset's gold.

Carolyn was learning French and getting better and better each day. I was working several hours each day on a new collection of poetry (called *Paris*, of course) and a first collection of short fiction. Reading Simone de Beauvoir helped me to understand myself as a writer and my own limitations, which was something I had failed to do for too many years. Now that I am approaching the age when most writers have their best work behind them, I feel that I am only just beginning to find my own peculiar style. Simone had written of her frustrations in trying to structure several stories so that they would stand as works of art. Intent, structure, style, tone—all had to mesh before she would call it done. She had finally abandoned several attempts out of sheer frustration, out of a very human inability to keep out emotional autobiographical content. The problem with my contemporaries who were now publishing, and in many instances widely, is that they make no real attempt to separate the personal from the fictional, no attempt to keep the memoir separate from the fiction.

At the Coupole

Free from the rain and autumn wind,
we settle into the booth shoulder
deep to slowly drink the dark tea
we know will save us from the colder
infected world of Champs Elysées.

The afternoon is heavy with
cloud and shadow. We see the ghosts
of those who had the will to stay:
Gertrude Stein, who praised Pablo most,
and one who looks like Hemingway.

Somehow we feel secure, cushioned
here in the brown-tone room where smoke
drifts like disembodied saints, where
the echoes of Joycean jokes
and Proustian narratives stir

such a bowl of memory that
we are swept away from our common
lives: we are exiles, and free.
Their presence falls like a summons
to the heart that reads simply *Be.*

We are ourselves and others, too,
for all that we imagine takes
some shape in the long course of things.
Fitzgerald enters in the wake
of Zelda. Outside green neon sings.

I have written on the problem of the personal in today's
fiction and have spoken out against pretentious self-absorption every chance I have had (often by means of rejection
slips), and reading Simone de Beauvoir in Paris brought
home to me the problem once again: no truly good writer
can discard or neglect the personal, but every good writer
knows that the personal has to be molded into something
that it essentially is not or was not in order to be art, whether
fiction or memoir. The lobster following Sartre had to be
exorcised before Sartre could enjoy the walks with Simone
through the mountains of Bavaria or through the gorges of
the Tarn.

Paris is always an adventure. Though we know what to expect, there is always the unexpected. We had bought a map of the cemetery of Montparnasse and were walking slowly along the avenues of the dead. From time to time I would point out the tomb of some literary figure (Saint-Beuve, Beckett, Tzara) I remembered from my college studies. Carolyn had a look of wonder on her face; so many great writers, artists. (Where is Man Ray?) I had to apologize for not being able to relate more of the writers' lives and works to her: I quite simply had forgotten too much. Near the cenotaph of Baudelaire, which seemed to be hanging from the high stone wall of the cemetery, two lovers were locked in embrace on a bench and were aware of nothing except their passion.

Carolyn touched ceramic flowers on the tombs of the ancient dead and whispered of the artistry and beauty in them. The camera swung from my shoulder in rhythm with our walk and we went hand in hand past the monuments, making our way to the section where Baudelaire is buried in the family tomb. Several yards from the tomb itself, we saw a middle-aged Asian coming toward us up the paved incline. He too had a camera slung over his shoulder and

was looking directly at us. When he was about ten yards
away, he suddenly pointed to his left and said, "Le tombeau
de Baudelaire." We exchanged greetings, in French, and
then he passed on. Looking back we noticed that he was
limping slightly, and when we looked again he was gone.

At the Tomb of Baudelaire

The guard at the main gate smokes a blond Café Crème
and contemplates the wind in the canopy of limbs

above our heads. We walk the wide avenue that all
the dead have ridden before, read the names that have
    taught

us mortality. Nothing about this place seems dull:
the stone flowers have a luster that grows full

as the day goes down. In lengthening shadows we ap-
    proach
the tomb where Baudelaire's mother laid him out of reach

of creditors and fools. Sunlight motes our faces.
The wind has caught the clouds: we know we will have
    to race

the November rain if we don't leave soon. Moments
before we turn to the tomb, a tourist with camera and
    lens

in hand, coming toward us a dozen yards away,
points left and says *le tombeau de Baudelaire*. No way

can he know what we are looking for. He smiles,
dark and oriental. On past us up the hill,

he removes a pebble from his shoe. The wonders
of Paris we came to see and all the walks under

the chestnut trees will pale beside what we recall,
years from now, of the small man limping toward us all.

How could anyone have known we were looking for
Baudelaire when there were so many other reasons for being
in the cemetery? The rich and famous of Paris and the world
are buried here. For us, for the moment, it was curious only.
That the Asian had known whom we were looking for was
not possible. Or was it? we would ask ourselves later, again
and again. Paris, after all, was a city of coincidences, a place
where you can count on recognitions.

We walked on after taking several photographs of the
tomb. Near the gate opening onto Boulevard Edgar Quinet
we found the tomb of Jean-Paul Sartre and were surprised
into remembering that Simone de Beauvoir was buried with
him. How could we forget that picture of her seated and
mourning, supported by friends in her old age, at the grave's
edge the day they buried Sartre? Flowers of all sorts lay
scattered about the low stone and the shells of several small
crustaceans. Sartre hated crustaceans; therefore, someone
hated Sartre, I reasoned in my poor logic. We sat on the
bench in front of the tomb and reflected upon our stay in
Paris and our visits with the writers we had read or were
reading now that we could visit the city with some regular-
ity. As I rose to stretch the pain out of my joints (we had
been walking most of the day), I noticed a coin beneath the
bench and asked Carolyn, who was still seated, whether she
had dropped the two-franc piece. She picked the coin up,

then rubbed it clean and handed it to me. It was an American
quarter. Proof of another pilgrimage or payment for time
spent with Sartre and Simone.

Meeting Susan S. at Musée de l'Orangerie

The same sad hat, the same white gloves,
she wore those days in Bellagio.
The same sad eyes, disdaining loves
she may have left in Menaggio.
An accident we saw her at all:
she was slow to confirm our call.

Oh, there you are, she said, as if
we hadn't been. Looking over
our shoulders, to the right and left,
she critiqued Monet's clover
and trunks of trees whose tops she could
not see. But the light on lilies was good.

Light was indeed good everywhere,
especially for Monet and now
for us, washing Paris in an air
framed by clouds and endless rainbows.
We had had a premonition
earlier we would see someone.

She paused, her eyes drifted about
the walls as if she expected some
reveling satyr to step out
of the maze of color and claim
his prize. We gently eased away.
She floated out into the day.

The coin gleamed when I rubbed it on my pants leg. I gave it back to Carolyn. She said that we would keep it with us for the rest of our lives. The traffic on Edgar Quinet had begun its late afternoon clamor, but we did not mind. We would walk across to Boulevard du Montparnasse and pay too much for an *expresse* at the Coupole or one of the smaller cafés and watch the Parisians dressed in perpetual black lean against the November wind on their walk toward home.

In Café des Deux Cascades d'Aise

To dine in the blue
light, golden carp at our feet,
we must read kanji:

we must understand the smile
on the faces of strangers.

The weather in November 1992 was quite bad: wind and rain for the whole length of the two weeks we were in the City of Light. This did not, however, deter us from the streets. One day out of sheer spite for the rain and wind we walked from our hotel on Plaza Haussmann, in the eighth arrondissement, down rue Faubourg St. Honoré to rue Royal and Hôtel Crillon, reputed to be the most expensive and luxurious hotel in the world. Though we never were guests of the hotel for overnight stays, we always found ourselves welcomed brightly by the doormen and others. The Crillon is a quiet oasis in a noisy city, and what can often be a cold and wet noisy city.

The *rez-de-chaussé* bar of the hotel was recently redecorated by Sonia Rykiel in gold, red, and black. And in an attempt to recoup the cost of renovation, the barmen seem to want to make a killing off each drink served. In honor of Hemingway, Carolyn and I each ordered a fiery glass of kirsh and sipped it for over an hour hoping the rain would end so we could continue our walk across the pont de la Concorde and down boulevard St. Germain to the heart of the Latin Quarter.

Looking for Hemingway's Ghost at the Crillon

When he was flush he drank at the Crillon,
by his own admission. We try the kirsh,
the cherries blooming down our dry throats
after a day in the Tuileries. A bush
coat hangs on a peg behind the bar Sonia
Rykiel redesigned. We know it could not
be his. But its hanging there blurs the gold
and red of the barroom and tells us older
tales than we hear across the bright tables.

Many a boast and bad lie still linger
in the whiskey air. We pay him homage due
and disregard the lies and lives he led.
His words do not mean trouble here: no one
reads in the glittering light lesser lives have
left. Ghosts still walk these halls looking for a way
to lose their sins. We raise our glasses to
all returns, liberations of every sort,
remembering hard the early days before

we lost a generation of giants who will
not walk these vivid halls again. We fool
ourselves into other lives, our own too
poor to rival reality. Our day goes down
heavy with wishes that cannot stand long
against the sunlight splashing through the panes
that speak across the years we do not know.
In our lives there is a vagueness no song
can make clear, nor utterance long endure.

   By the time we had finished the drink it was clear that
the rain would continue throughout the day, and though it

was good to sit there rethinking Hemingway's many Paris lives we needed to continue our planned walk or face an even colder night. As we had discovered, the Paris November days were short: it was full night by 5 P.M. on cloudy days. Paris is, after all, on the same latitude as Nova Scotia and insular Newfoundland. We were determined to walk and enjoy it.

By the time we reached St. Germain des Prés the night was heavy with rain and endless traffic. Then suddenly our sidewalk was blocked, cordoned off by a police barricade of some fifty yards or so. We made a detour left on to rue de Buci, then right on to rue de Seine, which took us back to St. Germain and the other side of the barrier. A crowd of three or four dozen people ranged along the rope and even out into the street, despite the heavy traffic. Everyone seemed to be looking toward a doorway next to a pharmacy, its green cross stark against the night. The crowd seemed uncommonly quiet. I asked a young man who was by the barrier, "Qu'est-ce que se passe?" He answered that an important dignitary was giving a talk upstairs. We thanked him and continued on down the street to boulevard St. Michel, and then ending our walk, finally, at George Whitman's Shakespeare & Co., next door to the oldest church in Paris, St. Julien le Pauvre, and under the watchful towers of Notre Dame.

Shakespeare & Co.

St. Julien le Pauvre stoops in shadows that lean
toward Notre Dame. The park grays in the rainy
twilight. Next door George Whitman's crumbling store

is the color of ashes and carded tomes thumbed
into oblivion. Two pigeons come
to the door, their bookish eyes red and sore

in the November rain. Humble they move aside,
as if we were masters here to provide
their daily bread. George stamps *ground zero*

inside the Gertrude Stein we pay too dearly for
and offers us a room for the night or
the week if we wish it. We do not go

upstairs. The recent fire has left a thin smell of
smoke everywhere. We hear the rattle of
teaspoons and cups. Small talk of poetry

tumbles down the steep stairs and hides under the lower
shelves, duller than ash. Outside the rain pours.
The pigeons trundle dead weight under trees.

It is not the best of times, yet we hold old books
with a joy beyond belief: we will look
through volumes to find what we hold no more.

We were dead tired by the time we reached George Whitman's shop, and after having dinner at Café Hamadi we
took the metro to St. Phillipe du Roule, two blocks from our
hotel. When Carolyn turned on the television for the late
night news, we were surprised to see very much the same
scene on St. Germain that we had witnessed a few hours
earlier. The only difference was that on the news the thresh-
old to the courtyard door, number 114, was heaped with
flowers of all sorts.

114 Boulevard St. Germain

November night. Wind and rain in
our faces and we walk along
boulevard St. Germain. The wind

shows us little mercy in its
rush westward toward some event we
cannot foresee. Today's news that's

on the air speaks of Yves's demise,
his great career and mourning fans.
We do not understand the police

cordoning off the sidewalk beyond
St. Germain des Prés till we see flowers
by the closed townhouse door, the fronds

of fern spilling over into
the pharmacy next door. The widow
grieves upstairs, someone whispers through

gloved hands. Video cameras roll.
We queue up to sign the black book
others are writing in. The toll

of churchbells is muted by clouds.
We write our names as if we are
petitioning for years. The crowd

grows. Faces seem familiar.
The green cross flashes on and off.
We leave our flowers by his door.

Yves Montand was dead. We knew his work, had seen
him in a recent film, were sad at the loss of his art and his
humanity. All those times that we had walked below his
apartment, and only at his death could we wave hello and
good-bye.

The next day the sun was shining brightly. We stood in line at the police barricade for an hour for the privilege of signing our names in the large black funereal book provided by Montand's widow. By the time we signed there were a hundred others queued up behind us.

Part of the joy of Paris is discovering those places that other writers and artists have loved so well or hated so vehemently. Whether you sit in Café de Flore or Les Deux Maggots or walk the rue Jacob, you do not, if you are a writer, escape the aura of those who have been before you. *Rive gauche* Paris in particular does not let you forget. Whereas American cities seem to want you to lose the past and join the mighty now, Paris is a monument to what has been.

After the Parade
> *14.vii.91*

1. Square du Vert Galant
The clouds lift under the slow swell
    of wind off Montmartre.
The Seine is calm now. The long day
    shades the spires of Notre

Dame, and the Conciergerie stands
    as silent as the sins
that stain the racks below the water
    line. The stairs descend

at Place du Pont Neuf where lovers
    lost their heads in other
wars once upon a time ago.
    This July the weather

smells of desert storm, oases
    blasted, a heavy wind
come and gone. The square's grass is green
    with lovers leaning, skin

bare to belts, and breasts calling to
    the sun in such a way
the air grows warm on this island
    near the end of the day.

2. Place St. André des Arts
The sun is down. Night shadows fall
    about us like light ghosts
no one can find heads for nor all
    the names. The final boast
of some dark officer, a call

that wiped the city clean of Jews,
    echoes through alleys that
we walk more softly down than do
    revelers from rue du Chat
qui Pêche. The day has seen a mood

not all are party to. Someone
    in black is reading from
a bronze plaque across rue Danton,
    the words low and solemn,
in the dim light of the metro sign.

There's a sound of weeping in the bells
    we cannot trace beyond
the loud fountain of St. Michel.
    Too many of the dead
haunt this place where resistance fell,

too much blood turns these cobblestones,
    too few stand silent here.
There's dancing in the street, the tone
    sharp and rocking clear
of traffic noise to the Pantheon.

3. *Place de la Contrescarpe*
Just steps away from Hemingway's
    room, near the top of the hill,
we take Tunisian tea. A spray
    of mint and pine nuts fill
every glass, the sweet liquid still
    the best drink of the day,

any day. The owner brings chairs
    he'd stacked so he could mop
the sidewalk late. The sky is fair
    tonight: wheeling stars stop
long enough for us to take up
    the cooling tea and care

that we are doing exactly
    that and in time and space.
There are ghosts waiting to be free
    from the neighborhood. We face
them at every turn, their cases
    pending, their trials to be

held in the higher courts of art.
        Ghosts and names linger long
on this low hill. Café Decartes,
        Café Lamartine. Along
rue du Cardinal Lemoine, among
        the day's trash, discarded

clothes from another age wait for
        a ragpicker who's slow
to come. The tea evokes still more
        than we can ever know
in full: the art of others flows
        out from every door.

This must be why we linger here,
        though we ourselves are what
we are waiting for, for we are
        the body and breath, not
lost souls, that taste in the hot
        tea all mysteries of art.

What Gertrude Stein and Alice B. Toklas began on rue de
Fleurus in the early years of this century reverberates still
through the annals of American literature and the culture
of Paris. Their salon gave sustenance and hope to many a
young writer, painter, composer, sculptor. Stein had an eye
for greatness and an equal eye for pretense. She knew what
it was to attempt a beginning, knew too that perseverance
was the better part of genius.

She knew beginnings were crucial in art, and those whom
she took under wing were better for the nurturing. In a time
when she is hardly remembered in America, except perhaps
in a rare university course, she is still much revered on the
continent of Europe. As late as February 1995, after a joint

reading with my friend Dagmar Nick, whose work I have
been translating since undergraduate school, a young slam-
poet and a native of Munich bent my ear with the words
"We must not forget Gertrude Stein and what she taught
us all about language." My reply was an incredulous
"You've read her?" His answer was simply "Hasn't everyone?" It was not easy for me to explain to him that in America
hardly anyone cares, including contemporary poets.

On Rue de Fleurus

With the garden in view at the end of the street,
we slow our pace to check the numbers on courtyard
gates. Across the pavement two lovers lean hard
against the door of a Peugeot. Street wind swirls dust
about their hair. Stein would have written a vignette
in another age and Hemingway would have corrected
proof. The best I can do is make a mental note,

which I doubt I will ever regurgitate. Poems
are tumbling down the rue I'd like to think, but what
it is is waste from flats now let to businessmen.
Rue de Fleurus is still at twilight, the lovers holding
the long embrace as if to stay time. My love
and I pass on, then double back, to make sure we
understand what we think we feel: a presence of

the past—in the dark windows that will grow bright
any moment now, in the courtyard that will blossom
with the night and the dinner guests arriving arm
in arm, in the street where still the lovers kiss.
In the growing dark the houses are as solid as a block
of print. This is where it was and is, a flowering,
a shining. 27, rue de Fleurus, and she never

locked the door in all those tumbling years when raw art
was gnawing at her heels. She loved it, was true to it,
and true to Alice B. My love and I give her
a long salute, would touch her door but for the lovers
straining still against the Peugeot, as they should be,
reverent only to their passion, their need to hold
the day in a purely personal, unassuming sway.

There is always a great stack of copies of *The Autobiography
of Alice B. Toklas* at George Whitman's Shakespeare & Co.,
as well as a plentiful supply of *Three Lives*, and now and
then even a rare volume of her work is unearthed. Being a
genius was not easy, Stein said. You have to modify that
nowadays with this: being remembered as a genius is even
harder. But Paris would not have the world forget.

Every arrondissement has its bronze plaques and often
in unlikely places (above the door to a bistro, under a second-
story window), lest the rest of the world forget: "Proust died
here," "Pascal wrote in this room," "Pablo Picasso's studio."
Marlene Dietrich, though buried in Berlin, is remembered
on avenue Montaigne, where she lived her last years. At
times you would swear that Paris forgets nothing.

Marlene Dietrich Est Morte

Now Marlene Dietrich is dead,
her flat at 12 avenue Montaigne
emptied of last light and the rays
of fame pinned upon the shabby walls.
For twenty years she took no calls,
walked only nights when the sky was lead,
recalled the dreams that would never stay.

Some lives we never understand,
nor were meant to. It's just that we
sense the diminishing, the freed
soul taking in its wake the space
she once occupied with a grace
no one could touch. A slender hand
on a slender waist, hair flying free,

whatever she played, she was Marlene—
rebel, mistress, whore, confidante
to stars and kings. All the dauntless
roles she replayed in solitude have
blurred into the shadows she gave
her late life. Too many ghosts lean
out from the graying walls to haunt

moments we try to remember the parts
in black and white. The film reads *finis:*
she stands before us, beyond us,
smiling a last good-bye before
the light flicks out and the night pours
in. On the street below, cabs start
honking the news of her demise.

One of her own that Paris remembers well is Victor Hugo,
with one of the longest spikes of Étoile (avenue Victor Hugo).
His villa is listed on the Michelin city map, and near it is
the Place Victor Hugo. His townhouse on Place des Vosges
is now a much-visited museum.

How many of us in America have read *Les Miserables* or
Notre Dame de Paris, to say nothing of the *Preface to Cromwell,*
the manifesto of Romanticism and the announcement of the
new age of poetry to come? We do not pay our debts very
well. Instead, we too often credit ourselves with what comes

from others. Not long ago, in a lofty university in Ohio, I heard a contemporary poet credit Walt Whitman with inventing *enjambement*. I do not think the Ohio poet would fit into Gertrude Stein's definition of genius.

Place des Vosges

All about us the toilers of
the street sweep back years. The roofs
are tile, drumming low under clouds.
Hugo's house is quiet at noon,
the voices of the nursery school
next door pool into light. Loud

streets seem far from where we stand
looking out into his garden
where now the roses are in bloom.
Summer day, summer day, sparrows
sing. Brown, dull, his paintings zero
in on all those common glooms

we learn too late that art is made
of. The sad shadows that he laid
on his work fade into now,
and we know him more than we would
by the words alone. It is good
to feel wooden brush below

his bust, the palette and the quill.
We never loved him much. The will
he had to work fills our eyes
later than it should. We owe him
a light we must not let grow dim.
We limp into art. He flies.

And there is also Notre Dame. For the people of Paris, the church itself conjures up fictional memories originating in Hugo's towering novel. Quasimodo is more real than history itself. For a fee of a few francs you may make the climb up the torturous steep stone stairs and view his favorite bell, now apparently silent forever.

Quasimodo's Bell

The climb takes you past the doors
no one has opened since war
rusted hinges and drove doves
into the rafters above
Quasimodo's bell. The bone
clouds cover the daylight moon
above Bois de Boulogne. No
calls of any birds echo
in the empty space between
gargoyles on the edge, the mean
faces full of vinegar
and pigeon shit. The haze for
miles shrouds the city at noon
so that shadows blend with stone,
and the gray air starts to hum
with a history no one
has told in odd or even
verse. The sky holds no heaven.
The sun continues its fall
fade. You want to weight the bell
in terms of human years, feel
the iron humps of backs it
took to keep the ringing fit
for knaves and kings. The metal
vibrates under your hand, all
the fingers absorbing shock

after shock of songs unlocked
at the heart of the bell when
Quasimodo fell and heaven
fell and rich men stole gold
from the poor and God was cold.

There was no way that I could visit Notre Dame without
writing about it in some form or another. It is just too much
of an art form itself for a writer's mind to put aside for long.
On first seeing the church, I had a desire to *do* something
for or with Notre Dame. It is a desire that is still there even
after the better part of a decade and a goodly number of
attempts to satisfy it.

Vision and Prayer
       Notre Dame, 12.vii.91

I turn no corner of prayer burning,
with a light given only toward
dawn of others' eyes, ring
hands emptied of hoard
and spittle. Bring
water or lord,
light sung
chords
or
boards
with sting
of steel, cord
hemp weeds gagging
into a hangrope adored
by dumb and honest singing
folk, and you will see ignored
by fat lips words I silently sing.

Without malice and madness, I hand
  you these words ground all day
    by throat, teeth, the sand
     in my guts, blue decay
      of gums, mucus and
        spit. On Cité,
         bottomland
          poetry
           re
         augury
       from hands
      roughed by hay
    and dirt and bands
   around the heart stays
  sharp, a plowshare to send
 sinking into a dumb world maze
to furrow a light line to the end.

    I am drawn to the literary things of this world. I saw
the Mirabeau bridge for the first time in June 1994. A new
acquaintance, Christopher Woodman, invited us for a sail
on the Seine in his forty-foot sloop, *Nausicaa*. Carolyn and
I had taken a tour boat a couple of years before and were
hardly impressed. But on the *Nausicaa* we cruised at leisure,
pausing wherever we wished from pont d'Issy, where Christopher kept his craft moored to a large barge, to the Musée
de la Sculpture en Plein Air. Apollinaire's poem immortal-
izes pont Mirabeau in such a way that I had to see the bridge
at some point, but I had put it off time and time again for
fear of losing the great feeling I had in translating the poem
in undergraduate school. In the red sunset of Paris, the
Mirabeau bridge lived up to every bit of the image and
personality Apollinaire gave it.

Mirabeau Bridge

from the French of Guillaume Apollinaire

Beneath the bridge Mirabeau flow the Seine
            And our loves
        Must I remember them
Joy comes always after pain

            Though night comes and the hour chimes
            And the days pass away I remain

Let us remain hand in hand faces close
            While the tired tired
          Wave of eternal eyes
Passes beneath the arch of our arms

            Though night comes and the hour chimes
            And the days pass away I remain

Love flows away like this fleeing stream
            Love fades away
          How slow life is
How violent hope

            Though night comes and the hour chimes
            And the days pass away I remain

Though the days and the weeks pass
            Neither time passed

Nor loves return
Beneath the bridge Mirabeau flows the Seine

Though night comes and the hour chimes
And the days pass away I remain

The forlorn quality of the French verses is impossible to capture in any other language. Somehow, too, you are glad in reading the original Apollinaire that in a fit of pain and craziness—so the story goes—the poet dictated that all punctuation be removed from all his poems. The sense of flow that the poem gives the reader is Apollinaire's stroke of genius. No translation can do it justice, much less mine. Physically, other bridges on the Seine far outshine pont Mirabeau, though it is Apollinaire's bridge we always keep coming back to in song.

The songs of Paris's bridges alone could fill a mighty tome. In the heart of Paris, it is what we all do from time to time, tourist or native: we stand on the bridge and wave or dream, between *there* and *there,* and know we have a choice in which way we go.

Boating the Seine

The weather holds
    and the river moves sure of its pace
below pont Neuf,
    where the bookstalls flap in the breeze
and the poor dogs
    whine on their wiry leashes kept
taut far too long.

The sun glares off
    the wakes of drunken boats slipping
shallow hulls left
    and right to make the tourist think
the short ride long
    and the voyage worth the price he pays
and the photograph

a record worth
    more than any frame. Pont des Arts
swarms with children
    from the Louvre jabbering like monkeys
in a canopy
    above the heads of cannibals.
The gold of pont

Alexandre III
    outshines the sun and the beggars know
this is the place
    to be, invalids all and free
from daily lumber
    of the boats below and the river's course
to the dark wide sea.

Apollinaire
    knew the bright bridges and the boats,
knew the beggars
    on the shore as far as Mirabeau,
when boating the Seine
    meant more than simply seeing light
at war with light

and shadows that
    his artist friends rendered in browns
and blues. Sunday
    boating down the Seine was a trip through
the heart of things,
    the broken heart of Paris sutured
by stone and steel.

The first time we saw Rodin's garden it was pouring down rain, an afternoon of summer storm. As we walked in the main gate from rue de Varenne, a casting of the *Burghers of Calais* on the left and the *Thinker* to the right, the imposing structure of the former Hôtel Biron stood before us. It was not at all hard to imagine the lives that had frequented it. There is a scene from the movie *Jefferson in Paris* in which Jefferson steps out of a carriage in front of the hotel that is exactly right, such a timeless image the building remains. (Unfortunately for the movie the rest of the scene is post-Jefferson.) The great figures in stone of Balzac and Hugo are there in the garden, among the boxwood hedges, the Napoleon trees, and the graveled walks. The garden is a serene pause in the heart of the city. You are almost unaware of the frenetic activity of the millions of lives that are Paris, except for an occasional echo of auto horn that comes leaping over the high stone wall of the garden. You can understand Rilke's love for the place when he worked for a while as Rodin's secretary.

I think that of all the places in the great city, the one spot we want to be, more than any other, is Rodin's garden, especially when we are tired or depressed with the weather or the unrelenting crowds of people. For us it has always been an island of tranquillity. There is never a crowd, rain or shine, and the flowers seem to bloom year round. The same kind of contentment surrounds me there as that which

I feel on my native ground, at the upper ford of Holson Creek, in Holson Valley. There the tableau of calm water flanked and roofed by trees fills me with a feeling of warmth and reverence for landscape that very much resembles what I feel sitting in Rodin's garden. The trickle of water in the warbler's song and the rustle of leaves overhead are transmigrations of the spirit. There are moments that never end, but repeat themselves in mind or art, and for this I am grateful, and for this I am a poet.

Rodin's Garden

Entering in a rainstorm, thunder
jarring the cobblestones, we move
along the path to the *Thinker*,
bending still in ponderous thought
upon the pedestal. We shove

umbrellas into a wind heavy
with cries of schoolgirls come to sketch
the *Burghers of Calais*, their heads
set in wet despair no haughty
child with pen on pad will ever catch.

Beyond the old hotel the marbled
light off clouds shows a deeper scene:
two lovers embrace under a fabled
hand held lightly above the graveled
walk and low bench. Under hard rain

they are as fixed as stone, eternal
in this their kiss that knows no end
no more than Rodin's does. We turn
aside, knowing love and art depend
on moments that should never end.

Inside the museum stand figures
of praying hands and walking men
and lovers locked in time. Ledgers
of light through the foggy panes send
messages we cannot begin

to understand without error
and dread: something is vanishing
from our world. News of tomorrow
lies cryptic in tile, the finishing
touch we trace in the diminishing

window frost. All moments must end.
Rodin knew but refused to let
them go. He was uncommonly kind
to stone: it became soft as suet
under his hands. Out of Tibet,

Patagonia, Texas, or
Kush, we come to walk these grounds
where the stone figures still ask more
than we ever will, while all around
a white and silent peace abounds.

From our favorite hotel on Plaza Haussmann it is only
a short walk uphill to Parc Monceau. I like going there early
in the morning, a time usually that only a few strollers are
about, and these mainly English nannies pushing perambu-
lators or leading the children of wealthy Parisians. (The
eighth arrondissement knows no lack of splendor in its great
houses and apartments.) Most often I walk across boulevard
Haussmann and up rue Monceau to Place du Pérou, then
take rue Rembrandt to the little south gate of the park,
crossing rue de Lisbonne and rue Murillo on the way. All

the homes on rue Murillo look out over the park with their
broad third-story windows and balconies.

Carolyn and I often fantasize that, when we realize our
American dream of boundless wealth, we too will have an
apartment on rue Murillo or rue Rembrandt. Both short
streets radiate affluence and are uncommonly quiet, even
though both intersect with one of Paris's longest and busiest
streets, rue de Courcelles. To live next to Parc Monceau, I
am afraid, will remain only a dream in this lifetime. But
what's a lifetime for, except to dream? If you have seen
Monet's painting of picnickers in Parc Monceau, you will
have noticed the pinkish houses in the background above
the strollers and the flowers and perhaps will understand
that this is where we want to be, where we can see the
morning light on the flowers below and watch the play of
shadows as the sun goes down and, like the picnickers, have
time to forget the broader complexities of this life.

Fireworks over Parc Monceau

Mid-July. Midnight opens under low-slung clouds
in brilliant light, fireworks over Parc Monceau. Our
balcony six stories up floats in soundless white,
traffic mute, explosions too far away to pound

our ears. We remember what we have never seen:
Paris under siege, Luftwaffe bombs, the green
of the woods translated by muzzles of long guns.
Night brings it back and we are lulled to sleep within

safe hotel walls. The light that rocks us both has rocked
this town for a thousand years: echoes of falling mock
the politics of power. We think we have the sense
to know the curve of time as it loops lightly back

upon us in each slow flash. Nothing ever ends:
we repeat the worst of things. Whatever sends
us to our art sends us with horror in our heads,
the lightning words to burn into the hearts of men.

Fireworks over Parc Monceau and we lie in bed
watching the midnight clouds of bearable light spread
saffron sheets on the roofs of a Paris grown quiet
now. Tomorrow will open with the thunder of parade,

big guns in stiff salute on Bastille Day, and storms
of applause will hail the desert troops, thousands strong,
from Étoile to Concorde. We are moved by what we see
and the need to count the scars on the cobblestones.

It is easy to forget the suffering of the city in Parc Monceau.
There are no beggars here. Cripples are bright and the sad
cheery. Monet saw it as an oasis of light, a refuge for the
weary, a diversion for the rich, and thus it remains. But it
is more. For me, it is the place that, one cold November day,
when no flowers should have been alive but the pansies
were, I knew I would write a hundred lines for Paris, and
then, if I were lucky, a hundred poems.

Crown

You end the book the way that you began,
a handful of Paris both light and dark,
all you think you know well enough to start
a mime of things. Nothing ever scans

exact on Paris streets: a grain of sand
will work a cobblestone away. No art
is large enough to hold the broken heart
of Paris for very long. A shadow of a man,

the ghost of a woman gone, you can't expect
much more. The map is never any help,
nor brochures from the bookstore at the Louvre.

You walk the worn streets until something clicks,
until that tearing inside the ribs lets up.
You try to pull yourself out of the blues.

*

You have to try to write out of the blues
to get the last words right. Courtly Ronsard
knew nothing he had done in verse would scar
the beauty of the perfect poems. The tools

of trade you learn to lay beside the fool
you are and turn to the few true things that are
right for you: the hard facts, the words at war
with words. You also lay aside the rules

others made that don't agree with your touch
of dawn or darker doom. The Paris you
know promises nothing you can foresee

but only offers you a chance. A brush
glued to one hand, you stroke the sky into
a lighter shade. No Monet at Giverny,

*

that's certain. No, Monet at Giverny
would paint from a better light filled with hues
as soft as down. His line would not be loose
but would give the impression of being free,

each stroke a carnival of light. The trees
in Parc Monceau droop their limbs to confuse
lovers straining under the molted blues:
one leaf in their hair and the lovers freeze

as if discovered in deadly sin. Chances
everywhere to hold the day is what
you want. A white-faced mime is walking on

the moon. The embarrassed schoolgirl glances
at her friend. The street is a melting pot:
everything becomes a part of what is gone.

*

Part of what is gone helps to make things clear,
and how to capture that in word or frame
is what poetry remains about. The same
then is now and will be whatever year

you walk these streets. The sounds you want to hear
always come; traffic's grind and snarl, the lame
tap of cane, the spangled fall of hard rain
late in the afternoon. Paris is as near

as you can get to natural poetry.
Translation is all you need, from senses
into the spoken word, the written form.

You take your meter from the gravity
of leaves, the final falling that ends this
groping in the dark for the perfect poem.

*

The perfect poem crouches in its warm womb,
waiting to be born. At night Paris sings
a lullaby in light. You sway with things
you do not know the rhythm to. The room

you write this in can never be your tomb
the way the one on Hamelin was to bring
to end Marcel's good work. The poem rings
true at birth, or false. You cannot assume

a perfect form, a sound, a sense, each day
without walking far out into the world
that is this city where the final test

is made: you hear the night wind traffic makes,
brittle grass breaking underfoot, the slow swirl
of the Seine past eddies of the souls at rest

*

under Notre Dame. Eddies of the souls
of poems are frothing in your head, mouths
wanting voice with every whorling doubt
you have regarding images. The toll

is heavy: you are dogged by the guilt you show
there is no reason for. You wonder how
the washed-up bones of poetry could allow
such liberty as you would like to know.

You don't wonder long. Words become current.
You swim against the flow to gain the nether
shore where no one waits. You hear howling wolves

and the clang of iron gates and the different
doom or dread some sad voice begins to gather
for you alone. So this is how it moves

*

for you alone. It moves you with a hard
shove toward your final destiny, the failed
work, the uncaptured melody, the frail
effort. Still poetry moves you. The bard

in all of us would like to sing, be heard
before we fall completely down. The gale
force in voice you felt you had when you railed
against the gods of poetry is absurd

now that you finally see the crown is laid
at the feet, not the head, of poets worth
their ink. Paris has given this. You gain

no fame. You owe Paris what you have made.
To Paris you owe the promise to work
to end the book the way that you began.

Of the one hundred poems, eighty are completed, and
over sixty have appeared in various literary magazines. I
began them early in 1992, at about the time the University
of Illinois Press published *The Sawdust War*. The poems were
coming at a furious pace, so fast that I had to brake for fear
of hidden curves. This was never a problem for me: once I
have a frame of reference, I do not mind going days or even
weeks without writing. In fact, the intervals between days
of writing are needed in order that I have time to market
the work. The grunt work of submitting to the literary magazines (and subsequently of querying book publishers) has

never lessened in all the years I have been doing it. That I have published over five hundred poems in the last twenty years in nationally and internationally known magazines means nothing: it is still difficult to find space for poetry, for literary magazines can print only so many poems per issue. The *Chariton Review*, for example, devotes only about eighty pages a year to poetry. For each page, there are easily a thousand submissions.

The writing of the Paris poems was well underway in the summer of 1992 when I did a seven-week gig for the University of Maryland Overseas Division. I served as writer-in-residence to military bases in the Far East (Japan, Korea, Guam) where the University of Maryland offered creative writing classes. Carolyn and I, however, continued our reading of expatriate literature and our nightly discussions, which always kept retracing steps that we and others before us had made in Paris. We were sympathic with Anaïs Nin's lifelong struggle for recognition of her diaries. In fact, we found recent paperback editions of the first four volumes of her diary in a bookstore on Guam. (The likelihood of even a bookstore on Guam seemed remote.) Gertrude Stein and Henry Miller continued to hold our attention in Japan while all about us a deluge of television, newspapers, and billboards assaulted our senses with a mixture of kanji, katakana, and janglish. I told myself then that there was probably no one in the world who would give a damn today or tomorrow about what I was writing, but I also told myself that I did not give a damn who did or did not give a damn. I would write what I wanted to write.

If the West is bad about not caring about good literature, the East is worse. From Tokyo to Okinawa the bookstores we found mainly featured masterpieces of the world as comics. Even noted native writers such as Oë and Yasunari were offered as cartoons. No one, it seems, anywhere, takes time for good literature or artful recreation. Yet every corner in the cities of Japan has its pachinko parlor with its little pawnshop around back. Those we passed—and we passed plenty—were doing a booming business, with the sounds of bells and sirens and balls clanking and with the wide-eyed stares of fortune-seeking souls.

Fall in the Tuileries

The carp in the pond
are Japanese: katakana fins declare
war on the two tame ducks

paddling this round
and simple inland sea. Two lovers' chair
tilts dangerously back

over the drowned
pebbles but rights again to show the bare
reflection of breasts slack

after the done
embrace. Nobody lingers long to stare
into the shallow lake.

The lovers' sun
shines upon their backs, and the sky is clear
enough at noon to make

the schoolboys run
down the graveled way. Now last flowers rear
their heads for beauty's sake

    before the turn
of season, before the long garden blurs
    under November's wake.

    The trees have gone
to sleep early this year. Not one limb stirs,
    bark and last leaves as black

    as coats at pawn.
For the Tuileries in fall, the price is dear:
    winter is a hard fact.

Paris *is* a moveable feast. It traveled well with us during those weeks in the East. And it is with me still as I sit here in Missouri at the end of July 1995 under an oppressive heat wave in which the heat index rises to near 130 degrees. Yesterday, a six-pound terrorist bomb blew to smithereens a half dozen commuters and wounded scores of others on the metro, fifty feet below St. Michel, while the ever-present Peruvian band above played on. I am sure that Gertrude Stein would agree that there is a there there.

Scenes repeat themselves and take on a significance you hardly noticed, if at all, when the initial event took place. The scribbler that we saw last summer in Café de Flore at work on page after page in his notebook we considered a pretender. Now we rejuvenate him with more hair and see him true. The painter at the Coupole, easily identifiable from the brushes in his shirt pocket, is today a latter-day Picabia. Henry Miller still sits in the shade of the trees in Furstenberg Square. We remake the world each time we think it.

American Poet

The Select swells with smoke and light,
    and the poet inside
works hard to be something other
    before wheeling time rides

him down in the turns of winter.
    Off in the neon night

the sounds of destiny at war
    with will jar his senses
against the bones he tries to hold
    upright. Traffic fences
in light upon the panes. He molds
    his fingers round the bore

of a ballpoint and smoothes the pad
    as if to clear it of
a clutter of targets no one
    could hit. When smoke dissolves
shadow becomes distinct, the run-
    ning words a force the mad

aim has to reckon with. The wine
    grows stale as the words build
a castle in his mind, and no
    mere voice can shake the still
tension that he has come to know
    while others come to dine.

He sits where Sartre sat, the chair
    philosophic as concrete.
He will not waste the trip to France:
    his poems will compete.
The waiter will know him at first glance,
    the dignified gray in his hair.

I gave a reading of my work during the summer of 1990 at the Pompidou Center, sharing the stage with four other poets in the Petit Salon. What I remember most about the Pompidou is not the reading, which was rather a formal affair, a bit too stiff for my taste, but the André Breton Collection, a mass of memorabilia including manuscripts, sculpture, paintings, letters, trinkets, even Breton's beetle collection. There seemed to rise from the exhibition a sense of the surrealists that I had never grasped before, though I recognized early in our Paris visits that surrealism was still alive and doing well in the city. Many of Paris's finest poets still acknowledge the movement, or incorporate it into their own stylistic innovations or borrowings from others. One poet will cry out that you must be original. Another will shout *vive dada*. Another will imitate Breton and Emily Dickinson at the same time.

Surrealist Poet

Theme is short,
    a smashed apple
underfoot

    or a ruptured
watch, spring
        dangling
worse
than a participle

    under Dali's
sun. The first principle
        is trust

that things turn
    out right, though
nothing must

seem correct.
　The *mot*
　　juste burns

　holes
in his brain.
　Broken circuits
hang
　from his nose.

One of the poets on the program read for over thirty minutes until he was stopped by our host, a psychologist-poet, and chastized for taking too much of our allotted time. His response was that he was just coming to the good part and it would take another fifteen minutes. Another did a slide show presentation along with his reading: both slides and reading were incomprehensible in their unrelenting but misdirected drive for originality. So many of the audience began to leave that I began imagining the sound of one hand clapping. Little wonder poetry is getting a bad name in the Western world. Every poet wants attention, but few care enough about what it takes to earn it.

Bequest: Coat to the Pompidou

Having a lumped head but right mind,
I bequeath my coat to the Pompidou,
to hang flapping in the hot wind

rising from all the farts there to
view beadling André Breton. They'll find
it slick as owl shit, black as flues

in the Marais. I wore it, and I dined
in it, and I wiped my nose on it twice
in the Ritz the day I declined

the wine the crazy waiter tossed
the maître d'. Let it hang tough above
the *rez-de-chaussée* and the dead lice

fall on whomever they may. Love
my coat or love it not. Many a time
it kept licks off my tanned hide, proof

enough it ought to be enshrined
with the other worthless crap that we find
in the front plumbing and behind.

Item: the pockets will be bare
as a rat's ass, no francs, not one red sou,
not one token of payment there.

Bill Moyers's poetry spectacular, filmed at the touted
Dodge Poetry Festival and running on PBS in 1995, may
have been the final death knell for American poetry. Even
the French recognize that something is dreadfully wrong
with contemporary American poetry. Moyers's program
verifies it for them: with one or two accidental exceptions,
every poet Moyers interviews and tapes reading is saturated
with the self to a degree that not even those two arch-
confessionals Berryman and Lowell would tolerate it.

On the desk before me is a full-page ad (in a recent issue
of *Poets & Writers*) in which the magazine praising itself
gives six quotations from six of the many short stories it
has published over the last year. Three of these six short
excerpts are centered on "mother." What is surprising to

me is not the frequency with which I see short stories or poems that are centered on family—*relativism* seems an apt term—but that now magazines are advertising the fact.

In the course of a year, I probably read over a thousand short stories and ten times that in poems that are submitted to The *Chariton Review*. A while back I counted percentages for a month: over 91 percent of what I read began with (somewhere in the first paragraph, or first stanza) the phrase "my mother," "my father," "my son," "my daughter," "my brother," "my grandmother," "my uncle," or so on. In nearly as many cases, the phrase constituted the first two words of the story or poem. My conclusion was that almost every short story writer or poet was writing like every other short story writer or poet. And I didn't have to look far among the reputable national magazines to confirm that what I saw in manuscript was being published as well. On my desk are several stacks of magazines published over the past few years. By selecting one at random, I see the fall 1992 issue of one of America's oldest literary magazines. Of the seven short stories therein, five begin the same as those of my survey. What further disturbs me is that far too few of the stories indicate that the writer knows anything about form and structure—about complication, about the uses of irony, about vantage point, about tone. The stories and poems are, in effect, personal essays that simply start and end.

In too many instances, every day of the week, I read the sorry state of the American short story and poem in the magazines I either subscribe to or get as exchange copies. (Currently *Chariton* exchanges with over seventy publications.) Only a few of these have the editorial integrity not to follow the trend in publishing today that more and more seems to be the personal essay under the guise of short fiction or poetry—the personal essay that is first-person narrative, very believable because it deals with that with which

we all have some familiarity, because it deals with family.
I love reading good essays and respect the genre. But I
damned well like my short stories and poems to be otherwise
than essays on familial conflict, real or imagined. Form and
structure determine the art. The *how* is always more important than the *what*. Those writers not concerned with the art
of making are doomed to have only subject to work with.

The Sentence

On the desk is a cup which is empty.
I drank the last of the tea only a few moments back.
The cup is empty I say.
I want the cup full.
There is nothing to do with an empty cup.
I look for a tea bag.
There is none.
So strong is desire that eyes water.
No tea in the world.
All cups empty.
I have died for the want of lesser things.

The magazine in the ad proudly displayed the excerpts.
Three were from stories by internationally known writers.
I was curious about the magazine. I had not seen a copy,
though it has been on the market for at least two years. My
reaction to the ad was such that I wanted to see one, especially since I had just received a subscription form in the
mail bearing the same quotes as the ad. I sent the blank
subscription card in, along with SASE, with the following
message: "Send me a sample issue. I don't like the tenor of
the quotes you include on the flyer. It sounds like lots of
'relativism.' All best, Jim Barnes." A week later my note
comes back and along with it a two-by-two sticky sheet
with these words: "Hi—Single issues are available for $9.00.

Thank you." No signature. It's just as well. Any editor pushing relativism in an ad is jolly well accepting it for the
magazine. I'm biased enough already. I don't really need
my suspicions confirmed.

A few months ago I received a fast note from a Maryland
writer who was apparently very upset over my rejection of
a story and comments regarding the rejection. The note
reads: "I too am the editor of a national literary journal, and
a good story is a good story regardless of how many relatives
are in it." Whoever said otherwise? One risks hate mail if
one comments on relativism and other sacred cows, it seems.
It's a petty world with petty art only if we allow it to be so.
As editor of a literary journal now into its twenty-first year
of publication, I try always to be kind in my rejection of
work and in my critiques, but I never accept fiction or poetry
or essays that I do not like, regardless what the trend or
who the writer. Even though I do not know everything I
like, I do know a few things in this life that I do not like.
And one of these is most certainly the personal essay that
pretends it is something else.

Celebration

Posters of Rimbaud everywhere
in celebration of his death-
day tell us yet he lives. We care
too little for his work: the breath
of air he stirred is whipped away
by those who think that what they say

will get them more in their season
than Rimbaud had in his early prime.
We hail him nonetheless; the reason
the poems still live is less the time
and more the man. In this odd case,
it's more the boy who chose a base

attitude toward art, then left it
flat when the juice ran out, his blood
not up to the constant flow fit
for what he wanted to do: flood
the words onto the page, to rage
against the rules, against the sage

of France who never understood
the genius of his craft. It's hard
to think he would have made his road
easy to hell by staying, the mark
of Cain marring his delicate skin.
It's sad to think of failed Verlaine,

pistol leveled at the writing hand
he knew he could never beat. Rimbaud
knew when to quit. More than we know
who walk these same streets. A hundred
years and we praise him under glass,
precious few of us in his class.

For five months we lived on the northernmost shore of Lac Léman, in Préverenges, while I enjoyed a Senior Fulbright Fellowship at the University of Lausanne. In the mornings when the mist lifted from the lake and with the Juras to our backs, we could see the distant white cap of Mont Blanc and the French Alps. No postcard has ever done them justice. A daily journal of those months, from October 1993 through March 1994, reminds me of the absolute splendor of place and tranquillity of soul we delighted in during those days when all I was required to do, outside my limited duties at the university, was to write what I wanted at whatever rate I wished. We were also surrounded by an atmosphere of history and art, without its intruding upon our lives. The freedom to be in and of it, and at the same time out of it, was the perfect situation for me as writer and for Carolyn, ever the lover of the good life. I wrote four short stories and a double handful of poems that are as good as anything I have ever done, as well as continuing work on the *Paris* volume.

We were never bored with Switzerland. We took endless walks through Lausanne, with its maze of steep winding streets and alleys. We took the ferry again and again to

Evian-les-Bains, on the French side of the lake. We took the
punctual trains to Basel, Bern, Sion, and countless other
towns. Once on the way to the museum in Martigny we
missed our stop, and the conductor put us off at a siding
high up in the mountains between Martigny and the Great
Bernard Pass, where the next train down graciously picked
us up a few minutes later. Those few moments of majestic
crags and silence, with only the wind in the trees, afforded
us a pause I doubt we will soon forget: our place in the
grand scheme of things may not be as significant as we
would like to think. It does not take much of the landscape
of Switzerland to teach humility.

L'Exposition

A cold day in Martigny
and we come to see the work
of Marie Laurencin. Her
portraits blur into form, lurk

oriental and light. Some-
thing dark from the eyes holds us.
The pastels are smooth as dream,
the brush she used cream to touch.

All the eyes seem oval slants,
all the robes lent by the gods
long absent from this Celtic
place Romans built on. The road

in named us native as scree
above our heads. We feel stone
threaten the figures that her
light touch turned into a stone

that is hers alone, but know
that the flow of color will
remain glacial and frozen
into forms that open still.

Dino and Tony Bellucci were first our neighbors (in the
apartment building in Préverenges), then our good friends.
Dino is one of the world's leading authorities on sixteenth-
century Reformation history and most likely the foremost
scholar doing active research on the life and work of Philip
Melanchthon, who, were it not for Dino's essays, would still
remain in the shadow of Martin Luther.

Early in November the Belluccis invited us to take a day
trip to Avenche with them. Tony wanted to visit the grave
of her parents there and to show us her hometown. (An
accomplished pianist, she once gave a concert in the ancient
Roman theater in Avenche.) We were amazed at the town
that the Romans called Aventicum, where the first-century
amphitheater and the medieval chateau, side by side, domi-
nate the hill at the top of the town. We walked down the
steep steps that cut through the stone seats ringing the arena.
Looking back up was as awe-inspiring as looking down.
We pretended we could hear the clang of metal on metal
as the gladiators fought. At ground level in the arena the
stones were massive and scarred with centuries of weather.
It filled us with a wonder we found more satisfying than
anything else except the Alps themselves. There was, as
Dino pointed out, even a runway around half of the arena
that was used to herd the wild animals into position for the
gladiators to do battle with.

We climbed up to where the château of massive limestone
and sandstone thrust its turrets as forcefully up as the Roman
theater spiraled down. Beneath one of the turret windows
a date: 1574. Carolyn wanted to know who lived there now.

There were flowers in the window. We could not tell her. I wrote a few words in a small notebook, the date beneath the window and something I remembered about the Château de Chillon, near Montreaux, and we walked over to the low west wall and looked out across the valley where the fog had begun to settle.

Leaving Chillon

Something dark stays with you on leaving the Château
de Chillon, not the memory of Byron's name
graved on the column where Bonnivard was chained
    below
nor the fog that rides the surface of the lake. The lame
gatekeeper gives you the evil eye when you go
past the stile and leave no Swiss francs. Not the same
dark that you know from deep night but the dark of
    threat
that is dreamed palpable. The history of sweat

and blood, the prisoner chained for years, the holy war
between the towns, all this falls away, but the stark
    weight
of Chillon bends your back for miles along the shore.
You try to shake it from your thoughts, consider shades
of trees at water's edge, or roses that are more
at bloom than you have ever seen up the brick way
to Villa Isbelle. The monkey trees and palms
are darkly green, and gloaming Lac Léman is calm

in the growing fog. You speak and try to calm your mind.
No one is near except the birds. You say a verse
or two from Byron's poem, something like *strove to rend
my bonds,* and stop. You have lost nothing here from first
to last visit. All is fictive, a sham of mind
you walk into along this promenade. The birds

are quacking at your loss of sense. Dark in low flight,
Chillon hangs above the lake, below the coming night.

Later we would drive down the hill and into the site of
the Roman forum, where a few remaining traces of columns
and walls could still be seen. But at the moment it was the
view from the wall that held us: far below, tiny cars and a
train were racing down the valley to some unknown destination, all as if it really mattered that they had somewhere to
go and needed to get there on time. Carolyn and I held
hands like young lovers, even though we were not so
young anymore.

The château towered over us, but we did not feel threatened. It had its place on the hill, and we would not argue
with that, no more than we would with the amphitheater,
although the thought of what had transpired in each left us
with a feeling of ancient dread. We stepped around a corner
of the château to come face to face with a monument honoring Swiss pioneers of aviation and now ajoining the château
a monstrous modern theater of glass and steel. *Mauvaise fois,*
Tony said. Bad faith for anyone to allow such incongruity
to happen. We turned our backs on the modern building
and the aviators, the only act of rejection we had at hand.
The château and amphitheater seemed to belong together,
regardless of their respective time and place.

We turned through a sandstone arch that came off gritty
on our hands when we touched it. Above a doorway into
the château, partially hidden by a twisting passageway, was
an ornate bas relief, the center of which was chiseled away.
It was what Dino had been wanting to show us. Once the
people of Avenche had been dominated by the Bernese,
who had built the château. When the Avencheans won their
independence from Bern, one of the first acts of assertion
was to chisel out the emblem of Bern, the bear, from the bas

relief. Art as such meant nothing to them, but symbol everything.

In the falling day, as the four of us joined hands at the Gatti graves, I felt as though we were beginning to understand, those few of us wherever we are, why the work has to continue and why it is necessary to get where we are going while there is still time.

We had taken an early morning train for Bern from Morges after having walked the mile down from Préverenges and our palatial apartment (our top-floor villa!) we had rented for the five-month residency. The fog lay in the valleys as the train wound through the hills. The hilltops and the mountains beyond were floating on a misty sea. Gulls from the lake added to the illusion of otherness. We knew this was something that would serve memory well in the years to come. We would never have enough of the Swiss landscape. We reached Bern at ten o'clock and took a bus to the American consulate, thanks to the guidance of Romi Berger, a colleague at the university. The conference on North American literature was to last all day, and scholars from Europe and Canada were delivering papers and deliberating as scholars do.

It was Saturday, and the city was milling with families despite the soft rain from the clouds that shrouded the city. Carolyn and I tried to listen attentively to the morning's speakers, who were giving a brief cultural history of contemporary Canada. The singsong of the voices was lulling, and before long I began to nod. Carolyn prodded me gently in the ribs, and I managed to open my eyes, several times. I suggested that we listen to the rain instead. We tried, but could only see it through the broad windows of the consulate's conference room. We both were worried that if the pace did not pick up the sessions would not be over before five and the shops would be closed. And tomorrow was Sunday and they would be closed all day everywhere in Switzerland. We had forgotten to buy bread on Friday, and now we would have none until Monday. "There are important things going on here," I whispered to Carolyn, to which she replied, "Yes, they are looking for their immortality and expect you to help them find it." The rain with its little fingers glazed all the windows.

Charlie and the Funicular

Rare December day: the sun breaks
into a radiance over Alps
few are witness to. The perched clog
car is almost empty. Knees ache
from the altitude and cobblestones. After over a mile up

you feel a need for valleys, fields
of grain and butterflies. Charlie
Chaplin lies far below. You can
barely see Clarens. My head reels
with a dizzyness comic and free
as a tramp in spring. Vevey and

Montreux are spread along the lake
under blue haze. If Chaplin were
here, the line would break, the clog wheel
slip from greased cups, and we would take
one hell of a ride back down to where
we started from, alive and well,

no worse at all for the fast fall down,
except hats gone and shirttails in
the wind. Funny how you can think
death would pass you by if and when
this or that were real. We begin
the descent and feel our hearts sink

at the thought that death could happen,
that indeed it eventually would,
in some form, comic or otherwise.
We come here to visit Chaplin
and ask for his forgiveness should
we think the world as simple as his

odd little Charlie Chaplin man.
There is no way to get away
from our piddling complexities
but to fall completely down. Then
who's there to care? We are not saved
even under stone and cedar trees.

When the meeting broke at noon, we had to decide
whether to have lunch or try to find a shop to buy bread.
Immediate hunger was most demanding. At the Tierpark
Restaurant, the group sat down to fried bread noodles and
venison in mushroom sauce. The red wine was excellent,
we both agreed. Four feminists were holding forth at our
section of the table, and it was difficult to say anything
without interrupting the discourse. But, since we were
seated across from each other, we did much commenting
with our eyes and brows on the nature of the dialogue.

Carolyn reminded me on our walk through the rain back
to the consulate that it would not be a good Sunday without
bread. I told her that perhaps the meeting would end before

five and we could get a good local product and bottles of wine before catching the train back to Morges. I should have known better.

The rain continued throughout the rest of the afternoon, and I could see the yellow leaves outside the windows of the consulate dropping one by one as they grew heavy with the rain. There was no reason for Carolyn and me to be there except that I felt I should, since I was one of the very few American writers in Switzerland at this time. It was not until all the sessions were over and the business meeting finished that Carolyn and I were formally introduced to the conventioneers. None of that really mattered to us, however. We were glad that it was finished and that important things could now be seen to—like bread.

We shook hands with three or four of the university professors, who made passing compliments about my recent work. But that, also, did not matter. On the way to the train station, a demonstration by Swiss farmers demanding greater subsidies blocked our way for several minutes. They marched slowly and ponderously: it was a synchronized march step, and each farmer had a giant cowbell, which he rang against his leg at each footfall. The clarity and monotony of the sound was pure raw power.

The rain set in early the day we boarded the boat for Evian-les-Bains. Carolyn and I were going across Lac Léman to spend the day with Jean-Claude and Diane Vicari at their villa above Evian. We had first met Diane in 1988 at a *rencontre* of French and American poets in Thonon-les-Bains, a few miles down the lake from Evian, and now were looking forward to seeing her again and to meeting Jean-Claude for the first time.

The rain was steady and cold and the November wind off the lake, though light, was chilling. On the hills above the port of Ouchy and greater Lausanne, the clouds were as low down as the Hermitage, where we had seen the Louedin watercolors the day before. I bought us camomile tea at the boat's concession booth, and we sat looking out at the waves in the rain and the splaying water. The rain hitting the water seemed to darken it. It seemed unusual that so few others were crossing.

There were over two hundred chairs on the lower and upper decks of the lake ferry, but hardly a dozen people were crossing over. Those on the upper deck, where we sat, all were busy writing in notebooks of various sizes or on single sheets of paper. I found it odd indeed: they did not

appear to be students. No one looked out toward the farther
shore except Carolyn and me, anticipating seeing the lights
of the casino in Evian. One of the passengers, a middle-aged
woman in a large sweater, rested her chin in her hand for
a long while, staring into the space of the upper deck, then
began writing at a very rapid pace and did not stop until
she had filled several pages. Probably the writers knew what
lay on the other side much better than we and had other,
more important things to busy their minds. But we had been
there only once before and for only a couple of hours. What
we had seen we had liked very much. We wanted to see
more of the town where the famous water came from. We
had a good laugh about it: we were going to the source for
a drink of water.

Evian-les-Bains for us was quite simply the other side of
the lake directly across from our villa where Diane and Jean-
Claude lived, and we wanted to see it more for that reason
than any other. I would write about Evian, or I would not.
It did not matter. It was what we would do. Nights, during
our walks down into Morges and back again to the villa,
when the lake was free of fog, we could see the lights of
Evian across the lake and wondered at its seeming nearness
in the dark.

The short ride across was as if we had embarked on a
long journey and the French Alps were a distant land that
we could never reach though the mountains loomed ever
closer. The gentle rocking motion of the boat on the waves
and the endless rain gave the crossing a dreamlike atmosphere. In the unerring motion of time, the thirty-minute
crossing in some other dimension could be an eternity. We
spoke of such things in whispers, though nobody was listening. Each of the passengers was hard at work on some
composition that had to be done before the boat docked.
Each writer had a seat and table apart. Only the two of us

were seated side by side, arms linked against the chill of
the day. We watched the passengers as the boat scraped
against the dock: each writer folded his leaves, put them
away, and walked briskly to the gangplank. In a moment
each had faded into the rain. On shore we stood under our
umbrella looking up the mountain at Hotel Royal, where
kings had golfed and queens lolled in luxury, a paradise in
decline. But we had made the crossing to spend only the
day on this, the other side.

Alpine Idyll

1. Gare de Lyon
At the station we waited for
hours, our patience running
with the changing times:

the train was late and then on time,
then late again. One beggar
knew us for fools

and kept coming back around. He
had a walkman on his belt,
snare drums so loud

they pounded our ears. Hip and mad,
he drooled on tables. The waiters
took hard offense
at his badgering us for coins
and apologized with their
open hands and eyes.

2. *TGV*
Minutes out we watch the landscape
blur. We have to look
at hills and sky

to keep the picture still enough
to think of France as new
country. No one

but us seems to care about
the shape of towns, livestock
along the fences,

and grapes rounding under Midi
sun. Already native enough
to keep the camera

low, I shoot my reflection
in the window and stop
the flow of meadows

on fast film. The day reels on past,
and the present vanishes
at the speed of light.

We reach Belgarde and change for the climb
that will be slow as mules
and tunnel-dark

to the top of the world where Romans bathed
and visiting writers chased
rare butterflies.

3. *Thonon-les-Bains*
The sky is blue, the mountains blue,
and the pigeons underfoot.
The lake country

surrounds us. We feel the glaciers' slow
slide into Lac Léman,
a solid gray,

and we want this journey to end
here. We want it to end
where the water's pure

and Hotel Terminus marks time
by the shadows on its wall.
The steeple clock

on the church is broken beyond
all Swiss repair. Still time
is what we have,

and what we want before we have
to go back down to catch
our running lives.

4. *Terminal Disease*
Five day, four nights, we calm our lives
with walks among the trees
Napoleon left

the country greening with, and dine
each night at the Savoie,
wine we only

dreamed before this paradise set in.
We are infected with
terminal disease:

we want to stay forever, here
where flowers bloom in mist
from the shaded lake

and our dreams enter through open
windows and we know nothing
will be this good again.

The Vicaris were wonderful hosts in the old French sense. Our "lunch" lasted all afternoon, so many courses that I cannot recall them all—the salmon, the fruit, the "ripe" cheese, the desert. Along with each course there was, most assuredly, a different wine that surprised our palates into a pleasure we will never know better again. Majeur, their German shepherd, kept us constant company throughout the long meal, nosing his own particular role into the conversation. (On our next visit, we would bring Majeur the largest rawhide chew-bone we could find in Lausanne.) Diane had visited the area as a student from the University of California–Riverside and had fallen in love with the country and Jean-Claude. After graduation, she came to stay and teach French and English in hotel management schools. Jean-Claude is a year or two away from retirement from secondary school teaching and is, as he puts it, now a happier man. Their home is a farmhouse (now their "villa") above the center of Evian-les-Bains, at Publier, complete with a double stone fireplace, opening onto both living and dining rooms, and exposed ceiling beams, a dwelling that dates back hundreds of years. The smells of wood smoke and wine and

cheese permeate your clothes and skin, and you leave feeling
that now you belong to this place.

Nearly all the days of winter along Lac Léman were mild.
Most times there was a soft rain along the shores. The clouds
shrouding the mountains, however, though not threatening,
let us know that a few meters up there was snow. Dino
and Tony spent several days of each week at their resort
apartment four thousand feet above Aigle. Skiing was in
their blood, no less than mountains are a part of mine. The
difference between the Alps and the Winding Stair is, of
course, enormous. Though on a smaller scale, my native
ground is still impressive to those visiting it for the first
time whose previous knowledge of eastern Oklahoma was
limited to John Steinbeck or others with faulty topo-
graphic perception.

On Blue Mountain Tower
for Jerry and Jeanne Easterling

Distance is blue, always: the hue
of smoke is a ghost of centuries
no lookout can ever know past fear.
You count this spot the loneliest
on earth and the best: not one sound,
save trees tell you you are someone
you have to be.

           The tower's derelict,
but legged enough to lift you over
pines into a wind you haven't felt
for years. The trail you see through haze
hasn't heard hoofbeats since your forebears
fought against the road the trail was then.

The river's dry, its blue a shadow
too thin to trace.

          You look at hands,
the only map you've ever known
you need. If you could read palms,
these hands would be this blue mountain,
that blue trail, that dry blue river.
But to count spent lead and broken flint
you know you need less blue and more
than valleyed flesh and warring bones.

Our own perception of Switzerland was completely
changed by the five-month stay. What we knew of the country had been little, except through encyclopedias and postcards. And I must admit that the postcards were more per-
suasive. Little did we know that it was a rich farmland. The
valleys were groomed and green with winter wheat, and
when we first arrived, in October, we saw great fields between Lausanne and Basel being harvested, with colossal
piles of sugar beets everywhere waiting to be hauled to
market.

Nor could we possibly have known that Montreux was
called "the Riviera of Switzerland." It was not until we
saw the palm and monkey trees and roses still blooming in
November along the shore's promenade between Montreux
and the Château de Chillon that we realized just how mild
the winter season was along the lake. There could be, and
often was, a sharp cutting wind from the north, but it seldom
lasted long enough to do real harm. Many times we would
take the train from Morges to Montreux just to make the
two-mile walk from Montreux to Chillon and back. It is not
difficult for me to understand why so many artists have
chosen to spend their final years along the lake. It is an

incredible beauty that meets your eye wherever you turn. Nabokov knew Montreux was a rare place on this earth. So too did Graham Greene and Charlie Chaplin: both owned homes in Vevey, just west of Montreux, and are buried there. So many others have been drawn to the region who surely must have longed to return. We could feel the eternal presence of young Ernest and Hadley Hemingway, of Jean-Jacques Rousseau, of Dostoyevsky, of Rilke, of de Beauvoir and Sartre.

Homage to Nabokov

The day is sharp with blades of wind thrown down
from the Bernese Alps, the glinting sun cruel
in its insistence upon an icy shine.
Today nothing happens above Montreux
except the roiling clouds and Norway pines
whose heavy limbs speak of memory in lieu
of snow. Yet as we enter the gate, the sound

of song flows down the hill from the gray fold
of Châtelard, where hands are pruning vines. Black
granite slab, a black stone lettered in gold,
the one last name. We come too late to ask
your pardon for the letter I sent, my old
request for your contribution, to which
Vera answered curtly, in type bolder

than my Royal's had been, that N. did not
send things for *consideration*. Too late
we know humility and the aching rot
of pride. Forgive me for my once rude state
of imbecility: indeed I did not
know your life. My wife and I hand you fruit
from the persimmon tree, its flesh a hot

pale fire on our tongues. There is no great risk
in eating the fruit in this graveyard: the frost
of November has cooked the skins and mist
from Evian has washed them clean. At most
we will stay an hour and feel we are blessed
to have leaned upon your good name, a host
of vines at our backs, and made our visit.

Wherever I go, it seems I never get too far away from home but what I am reminded of it. In Switzerland, it was the mountains, to be sure. But even more than that, it was my meeting with Ian Kirby, a professor of English at the University of Lausanne. We spoke briefly of our interests at first meeting, and Ian said that his abiding interest lay in runic inscriptions. He mentioned investigation he was doing on runes in America, in particular the Heavener Runestone (*Heaven-er*, he called it, though in the vernacular it is *Heevner*). I was stunned momentarily. Then when I told him I was born seven miles west, as the crow flies, of the runestone, it was his turn to be stunned. Voilà, a lasting friendship based on an alphabet we both understand imperfectly.

I was poor help for Ian in his research, but I was able to give him a bit of local color and legend relating to the Indian Rock, as residents of the Heavener area have long called it. I had even taken photographs of it in the mid-1960s while it was still in its wilderness state on Poteau Mountain, a mile up east of Heavener, ten miles northeast of the Winding Stair. My brother, Hack, and I had scouted the area several times when I was home weekends from college a year or two before it became an official Oklahoma State Park. I had even been so bold as to do a longish article for the *Poteau News* on the subject, but I soon lost interest, since graduate school in modern comparative literature loomed large on my personal horizon. The runestone has never, however, quite lost its mystery. There is something very old and even forboding about the broad eight-rune inscription on the tall upright slab of savana sandstone.

The Captive Stone
at Heavener, Oklahoma

Enmeshed in steel stands a stone,
near stunted ash and elm, cracked bones
of Yggdrasil, small trees of time:
the caged stone with ciphered runes
is part of park where men once made
their mark with maul and biting bronze.

The aged stone, hard to hand's touch
when touch was still allowed,
has had its face forced clean:
lichen lies dead below washed runes;
webbed shadows of encircling steel
now mark time on the lone stone;
yet the stone stands as stone stood
when Odin still was king and came
with men to mark down lives and fates.

Now we who Sundays look long
on this stone's stark ruined face
see only stone and ciphered runes
under the steel's sharp shadows:
the whispering of wind through wire
carries scant legend, no hint of history.

A year later, driving across the Winding Stair, on our way back to Missouri from southern Arkansas and East Texas, where I gave readings of my poetry, Carolyn and I stopped at the spot which once held the 100-foot Winding Stair forest lookout tower and took several photographs of Poteau Mountain. Fortunately, there was a thin thread of smoke climbing straight up from the runestone park. Thus I could pinpoint for Ian an exact birds-eye view of the position of the runestone in relation to a good chunk of my native ground.

All my colleagues at the University of Lausanne have become important pages in my journal of Switzerland. Besides Ian and his calm and cordial ways, two others in particular were more than helpful, erudite and at the same time full of humor and goodwill. Always available when we needed assistance understanding the procedures of *la poste* (where you pay utilities and rent among dozens of other bills), David Jemielty, an assistant professor and also a formidable bicycle racing competitor, gave us our first introduction to Swiss ways (no banking except long-term and credit cards). Peter Halter, acting chair of the English Department, made us feel at home from the first to the last, graciously inviting us into his home for a dinner of the famous Swiss *raclette* and thus giving us a farewell we will not forget.

We left Switzerland with much *mal du pays,* as Dino and Tony Bellucci say in Préverenges. A feeling deep in the soul that you are leaving something behind you cannot do without. Wherever you go, if you are a true human being, you put down roots into the earth you cannot pull up without pain. I confess I have *mal du pays pour la Suisse.*

The winter of 1995 was one of the worst on record for central and northern Missouri. There were over twenty inches of snow on the ground at one time in Columbia, where the University of Missouri closed its doors for the first time in recent history. Ninety miles to the north it was even worse, with more ice and far colder temperatures. Carolyn and I were, fortunately, away. We had been invited to spend the months of January and February at the Villa Walberta, on a hill high above the village of Feldafing and the western shore of the Starnberger See, as a translator-in-residence and guests of the *Kulturreferat* of the city of Munich. I had completed translating Dagmar Nick's *Gezählte Tage*, and Dagmar, a longtime resident of Munich, had seen to it that we were invited so that she and I could work closely on the final revision of the translation. (Five of her original poems with my translations follow.)

We left Lambert Airport, St. Louis, in snow and arrived in Munich in snow. In fact, it seemed a fullblown blizzard by the time we reached the Villa Walberta. If the *Kulturreferat* had not arranged for us to be met at the S-Bahn stop in Feldafing by Herr Hassler, the caretaker, we would have frozen to death in a matter of minutes. The wind blew continually, and it snowed intermittently for twelve straight days. We thought we were in for it. But then it stopped, and for the remainder of our two months there the weather was quite pleasant, with sun or soft rain, with only an occasional day of snow, and never very cold at all.

Flugwetter

Die Himmel dröhnen
Vergeltung.
Ein Schwalberwirbel
im Sog der Gefahr
ruft das Chaos aus.

Wir üben das Sterben ein
mit dem Schleudersitz
täglich und täglich.

Zweihundert Meter und
ein Grab tiefer:
wie tröstlich
das rote Kreuz auf dem Dach.

Wir kennen die keimfreien
Messer, den neuen OP
und die Riten
der letzten Ölung.
Manchmal erkennen wir beides
zu spät.
                                   —Dagmar Nick

Flying Weather

The heavens drone
revenge.
A flurry of swallows
in the slipstream of danger
exclaims chaos.

We practice dying
in the ejection seat
day after day.

Two hundred meters
and one grave deeper:
how consoling
the red cross on the roof.

We know the sterile
scapels, the new OP,
and the rites
of extreme unction.
At times we recognize all
too late.

Back in Missouri the glacial floe held everything in place.
But here we delighted in Munich and its environs. There
were only a few days that we were not taking the S-Bahn
into Munich to visit the great museums, especially the Neue
Pintakothek—the Alte Pintakothek was being renovated—
and the Residenz, or simply to walk the streets and gardens
of that great Bavarian city. Whatever anxieties we may have
had about Bavaria soon dissolved into warm realization
that here was country we could live in, given the time and
resources. But there is never enough of either.

Flug

Wie wir die Flügel jetzt heben,
wer weiß, in welche Gefahr,
welches Leben—und Überleben
jenseits von allem was war.

Durch Andromedas Nebelgewänder,
die Krone Ariadnes im Haar,
unter uns taumelnde Länder
jenseits von allem was war.

Spurlos, vom Sternwind umstoben
fliehn wir, der Schwerkraft enthoben,
in did wirbelnde Galaxie.

Wieviel Angst vor diesem Gelingen,
wieviel Zuversicht unter den Schwingen:
Jetzt oder nie.

                                        —Dagmar Nick

Flight

How we raise our wings now,
not knowing into what danger,
what life and what survival
beyond everything we know.

Through Andromeda's nebular robes,
Ariadne's crown in our hair,
below us countries stagger
beyond everything we know.

Without a trace, fanned by the wind
of stars, we take off free of gravity
into the whirling galaxy.

How much fear there is about this endeavor,
how much confidence under the wings:
now or never.

We devoured Bavaria, and yet we were never sated with
it. So much history, so much art. So much guilt, so much innocence.

The Villa Walberta is a haunted place. A quarter mile up
the hill from the lake, it looks out over the tops of tall
Bavarian pines toward the farther shore, clearly visible on
days when the fog of winter lifts. With the naked eye you
can almost see the small cross that marks the shallows of
the shore where King Ludwig II drowned. Proclaimed an
accident by his ministers, the drowning was likely the work
of foes within who considered Ludwig a mad king who was
squandering the nation's wealth on castle building: both
Ludwig and his doctor were drowned at the same time,
after having set out for a short walk along the shore.

It gave me great pleasure to stand on our third-floor balcony looking out over the Starnberger See and think that
quite possibly Eliot had stood there to find the exact lines
he needed for the opening section of *The Waste Land*. The villa
is now the property of the city of Munich, which, through the
auspices of the *Kulturreferat*, invites artists and writers to
spend time there working on projects related to the city or
its inhabitants. During World War II, according to the locals,
the villa was involved in medical research and experiments
in germ warfare, particularly in the study of malaria. Perhaps the story is true, perhaps not. But the fact remains that
the villa was built at the turn of the century by one of the

men responsible for developing quinine, a highly successful treatment for the fever.

Many a night during our two-month stay, I felt a cold chill creep up my back as I stood beside the washing machine and dryer in a gloomy basement room of the villa. The adjacent room was an enormous walk-in freezer compartment with a fisheye peephole in the door. The freezer was not operative, but there was always, for me, an eerie though calm presence in the basement that I could not explain. Slava, an artist from Kiev, sketched in black ink the semblance of two figures, male and female, floating above the villa and presented it to us on his departure for the Ukraine. He had captured in his art the essence of what I had felt so many nights in the villa.

Vorgefühl

Die Uhren werden uns überholen
an einem Mittag
im Herbst,
wenn der Rost von den Bäumen fällt
und das Blut,

wenn die Vögel mit ihren Schwingen
uns zeichnen,
Atemgewordene,
in die duldende Luft,

wenn wir den Stachel der Zeit
nicht mehr spüren,
Abend und Fortgehn,
dieses dauernde Abschiednehmen,
diesen Widersinn Liebe,

wenn wir, schwarz und vernichtet,
Gegenwart bleiben,
während die Zeiger über uns
wegrücken, als wären wir
nie gewesen.

—Dagmar Nick

Presentiment

The clocks will overtake us
some midday
in autumn
when the rust drops from the trees
and the blood,

when the birds with their wings
mark us
breath created
in the tolerant air,

when we no longer feel
the thorn of time,
evening and parting,
this constant farewell
this absurdity called love,

when we, dark and destroyed,
remain in the present
while the hands above us
move away, as if we had
never been.

The roads in Feldafing reminded me of the streets in
Tokyo. Even though they were marked, they twisted in such

confusion that any enemy would be moved to distraction when trying to find a specific house. More than once in the first few days of our stay at the villa, we were lost in walks down the hill. But that, too, was part of the joy of being there.

Thomas Mann spent several months in Feldafing working on *The Magic Mountain*. In 1919 he was invited by a Munich art dealer, George Martin Richter, to buy into property that Richter owned above the lake. Unfortunately, the house where Mann developed the character of Settembrini is now part of a communications complex. Settembrini would probably approve of satellite transmission, if not the material transmitted. I can almost hear him saying, to Hans Castrop, "Progress, Engineer!" This was not the Haus Berghof, but there was a kind of magic at work on the hill above the village.

My mornings were spent polishing the translations I had done of Dagmar's dark, sad poems and keeping a daily journal. From the balcony the lake lay gunmetal gray on heavy days and took on various shades of green when the sun struck it near the shore. Occasionally a lone winter fisherman would sail out to try his luck. It was an uncommonly mild winter by all accounts. Early in February Dagmar commented that spring could come any day but that we must not be misled into thinking that it would.

Am Ufer

Wir haben vorausbezahlt, Charon,
leg ab.
Eine letzte Münze
klemmt mir noch unter der Zunge.
Ein Bleilot. Die goldenen Worte
schenk ich den Lebenden.

Wir haben die Funeralien
bestanden, sind begraben
seit Jahren, Charon,
laß es genug sein, zerbrich
diesen schwarzen Spiegel.
Setz über.

—Dagmar Nick

On the Shore

We have paid in advance, Charon.
Shove off.
One last coin
still sticks under my tongue.
A lead slug. The golden words
I bequeath to the living.

We have made it through the funeral rites,
have been buried for years. Charon,
let that be enough. Shatter
this black mirror.
Take us across.

That the villa was a magical place to work is the way
Jachym Topol described it to us. His residency coincided
with ours, and he was deep into a series of short stories,
having just published his first novel, *Sisters*. He could sit at
his computer for hours and no one would disturb him. There
were only the wind in the pines and the lake beyond. So
very different from the hustle of his home in Prague, where
each day much time was spent in the cafés and with editing
his literary magazine, *Revolver*. So little time to write, he
said. But here, well, this was paradise, except for the price
of cigarettes (he smoked Marlboro).

Judah Ein-Mor, a photographer from Israel, echoed Jachym's feeling for the villa. This was his second residency. He had been living in Berlin for some years and recently was working on a large portfolio of photographs that made dynamic statements relative to customs and landscapes of different regions of Germany. The *Kulturreferat* held his work in high regard, and he had had several exhibitions in the Munich area.

On the night before our departure for Paris and subsequently home, Carolyn and I shared several bottles of wine with Judah and Jachym and, for the first time during the residency, discussed our work. We were joined by Barbara Radloff-Niggl, who lives just down the hill from the Villa Walberta. A photographer of international reputation, she had taken shots of each of us several days before. We all felt that we were old friends, though Carolyn and I had seen the other residents only at Tuesday afternoon teas and Barbara we had seen only twice.

Judah, Jachym, and Barbara are what I call honest artists: they do not feel the need to impress you with their work or erudition as do so many in America today. We sipped wine and ate cookies and fruit well into the morning hours in the grand sitting room of the villa. Before we said goodnight, we opened the windows and listened to the wind in the pines. Below, the Starnberger See was an immense plain of darkness. Each of us knew that we would not stand together at this height again, and there on the veranda of the Villa Walberta, a certain sadness came, then passed over us.

Abschiede

Auch die Abschiede werden jetzt leichter,
als wären sie nicht so gemeint.
Horizonte voll unerreichter
Hoffnungen—weggeweint.

Dein Winken zurückgeworfen.
Diene Händen versinken im Meer.
Kein Anker für meine amorphen
Träume der Wiederkehr.

Abschiede. Nirgends war Dauer.
Schon zerrieselt dein Aschengesicht.
Am Ende ist auch die Trauer
ohne Gewicht.

—Dagmar Nick

Farewells

Now even farewells are easier
as if they were not meant to be.
Horizons full of unattainable
hopes—wept away.

Your waving is thrown back.
Your hands sink into the sea.
No anchor for my amorphous
dreams of return.

Farewells. No continuance. Already
your ashen face sifts away.
In the end even sorrow
has no weight.

August 19, 1995, marked the end of an era in Summerfield, Oklahoma. On his birthday, at the age of ninety-six, Jack Curtis, longtime proprietor of Curtis Grocery, died. My first cousin by marriage to Lola (Aunt Mae's daughter), he was the last of the old ones in Summerfield. I can think of Jack and Lola no other way than as elder brother and sister, so close we were those years of my youth and adolescence. For fifty years, before retiring a few years ago, he made salami sandwiches (meat and bread only), sold everything from horseshoes to mothballs, listened to everyone's troubles from Red Oak to Poteau, from Talihina to Bokoshe, and persisted in keeping the general store the way he had from the day he opened it for business. The false front, the tin roof, the bare-lumber floor, the potbellied coal stove were what you expected when returning to native ground. It was difficult for him to close the store, but his eyes were failing so much that he could not recognize the customers, and that would never do.

We returned for his funeral on one of the hottest August days on record. The humidity was thick as soup: no one took twenty steps without sweating through his shirt. The funeral was an upbeat celebration of his life. Ben was determined that his father would not leave a saddened town and instructed the preacher and the choir to choose their pieces carefully. Ben himself gave the eulogy, and his wife, Judy, his sister, Ila Rea, and Lola smiled in sad joy below the cascade of flowers. The church was full to overflowing. I could see faces there I hadn't thought of or seen in thirty years. Later, outside in the reigning heat, I saw still others whom I had known well as a young man.

Standing in the shade of an oak at the corner where the churchyard touches the Bob Smith property were Sherrill Evans (a.k.a. Sundance, a.k.a. Bus-eye) and Neil White (looking more Choctaw than he had in his twenties when I last saw him) and his son Ruben, my grandnephew (whom I hardly recognized). I shook hands with Clinton Singleterry (a.k.a. Doc) and his wife, my cousin Bobbie, and chatted briefly with Kent (a.k.a. Clark Kent, Doc's brother, who was largely responsible for my enrolling at SOSU as a freshman) and Clark Nowlin (also a.k.a. Clark Kent, Kent's and Doc's brother-in-law, who had lost his wife, Suzanne, to cancer a few weeks back). The faces were the same, more lined perhaps, more fallen with gravity, but still the same faces that I grew up with on the hill that is Summerfield. It was, momentarily, as if I had not been away for thirty years, as if things were as they had always been, except for the old ones dying. Then I thought of Suzanne dead and my niece, Sue, dead at an age far too young, and clock time began to tick again. Evelyn Evans, James Hoot Jackson's mother, tugged at my arm and asked to be recognized. Lloyd Brannon shook my hand. Denver Evans spoke of old times at Dooley's Station. Jay and Juanita Burnett blessed me with their gentle ways. Tony and Nin Erle Barnes thanked me for poetry. These, my elders, too soon will be the old ones and another generation will have passed. Jack's life spanned four generations, all of which were represented in the celebration of his birth and death day.

After the burial ceremony, Carolyn and I walked through the graveyard to the Barnes and Adams family plot. We had not visited my father and mother's graves since they died, Austin in 1981 and Bessie in 1985. The cemetery seemed very small. I could swear that in my teens and twenties it seemed to cover acres of the hill above Holson Creek. Now the hill seemed no hill at all and the graveyard no more than a little pasture of stones. This final ground holds few of the family, my mother and father and

JOSEPH ADAMS   LALIE ADAMS
1903   1903

Nearby are CHARLES ADAMS and OLIVER ADAMS and MAE HAN-KINS and my sister Erma's daughter, my niece, SUE WHITE. A little farther on we read

MUREL KENNETH BARNES
1931

His had been a crib death when he was about three months of age. There is the haunting question at the back of my mind: if he had lived, would I have been born a scant two years later?

Autobiography, Chapter VII: Home for Memorial Day

The names that trust their bones to this hot hill
    have learned the rage of stone and pine. The wind
    that brings the morning into your eyes says live.
    You try a stone, find it rooted past your years.
    You question why you came. The answer comes out
    wrong as the women you haven't seen since hot sin
    was in your groin. *Belovéd, Gone From This World,*
    in weeds. Gold in a mourner's teeth names you fool.

Years past they used to spread a picnic under pines,
    sing hymns that sparked a bright beyond, and lovers
    rolled on stones and needles fierce to skin. You feel
    yourself in somebody else's dream: one friend whose
    hello is too far away to see, relatives too golden to
    touch, the *Requiescat In Pace* no foreigner can read.

You tell the fat friend you no longer know your life
    and see your epitaph in his handful of white roses.
    The way he hides his flowers behind somebody's
        name
    makes you feel the shame. His *Belovéd* cannot be read
    because of weeds. You want to touch his stone, tell
    him: we have endured. But you say something
        vague—
    yesterday's weather, God—customary words to exit
        on.

It was a dry time for Summerfield. Even the grass in the
cemetery had turned crisp and brown in the terrible summer
heat and humidity that only Oklahoma can know. Ticks
were everywhere and grasshoppers and snakes. Dust rose
from the crumbling grass as we walked back to the car.
Across the fence to the south, Waford (a.k.a. Stony) Evans's
ranch smoldered in the late afternoon haze. On the other
side of the county road, Booth Dean (a.k.a. Fad) Grey's
enormous log house tells us that nothing of any importance
has changed: in essence what we were we are and will be.
Everywhere I look are images that bring the past up to now
and signal the future. No matter how different I may have
wanted my life to be, what remains is the fact that I am tied
to this place, this blood, and this ethic that continues to
emanate from my native ground.

Lamentation and Farewell

A time
ago the time
to go seemed years away:
days were racked like cards on a tray,
face down

but full
of the high hopes
of jack, of queen, of king.
When we played high stakes, we played blind,
no thought

of what
lay before us.
We could not lose in such
a paradise as this with light
being

both par-
ticle and host.
That was a time ago
when the time had not come for us
to fold.

Now we
leave with spent hearts,
flat wallets, a gambler's
wish, but we were oh so rich
so long.